[1907]

New Poems

Rainer Maria Rilke

Translated by Edward Snow

North Point Press
Farrar, Straus and Giroux
New York

Translation copyright © 1984 by Edward Snow
Published in Canada by HarperCollins*CanadaLtd*
Printed in the United States of America
Library of Congress catalog card number: 84–060683

Third printing, 1994

North Point Press
A division of Farrar, Straus and Giroux
New York

Contents

Introduction

Rilke arrived in Paris for the first time in September 1902, commissioned by a German publisher to write a monograph on Rodin. He was twenty-seven, and already an accomplished poet with a considerable body of work behind him. In addition to the outpourings of his early years (nine books of poetry and fiction between 1894 and 1899), two of the three sections of *The Book of Hours* were complete, and the first edition of *The Book of Images* was about to be published. All this early work is unremittingly subjective; it still belongs tonally and texturally to the impressionistic, feeling-centered world of a late-nineteenth-century aesthetic. But what in the beginning borders on callow self-indulgence (one of the volumes of poetry is called *In Honor of Myself*) gradually deepens into a disciplined lyric temperament. The spacious, gently modulated rhythms of the first part of *The Book of Hours* are the creations of a poet who is very sure of himself; Rilke later said he could have continued in this style for the rest of his life.

But the move to Paris was to change everything. Shortly after Rilke arrived there, he met Rodin, and his interest in him soon deepened into near discipleship. As his enthusiasm for the sculptor's work increased, so did his dissatisfaction with his own. Rodin was a laborer, a craftsman, and the energy and dedication with which he immersed himself in the actual process of *making* seemed to Rilke a rebuke to his own lyric dexterity and slavish dependence on inspiration. With Rodin's "travailler, rien que travailler" ringing in his ears, he set about acquiring an entirely new set of working habits—forcing himself to write every day during regularly scheduled hours, wandering about Paris practicing the art of observation, taking notes, making lists of subjects for poems. Meanwhile he began to entertain the idea of a poetry that would answer to what he described as Rodin's "art of living surfaces"—a poetry that would somehow manage to belong to the world of things rather than feelings. The results—appearing slowly at first, then coming to fruition in an incredible burst of creative energy that spanned the summers of 1906 and 1908—were the two volumes of the *New Poems*, which together constitute one of the great instances in modern literature of the lyric quest for objective experience.

What specifically is "new" about the *New Poems?* The most striking transformation occurs in Rilke's language, which grows simultaneously more lucid and complex. Compression of statement and elimination of authorial self are taken to their extremes in the pursuit of an objective ideal. Only a few of these *Dinggedichte* or "thing-poems," as they soon came to be called, are actually about objects, but all of them have a material quality, and confront the reader with a sculptural, freestanding presence. Even their semantic densities communicate a sense of volume and contour. One is always aware of them as things made. Syntax, especially, becomes a tensile material capable of being worked into structures that remind one more often of the space-mobilizing forms of Arp than of Rodin's massive presences. Even in a poem like "The Capital," devoted entirely to the description of a static object, visual image interacts with a kinesis of line and syntax to make the thing come alive in the imagination:

> the vaulting's ribs
> arch out of the tangled capital
>
> and leave there, crowded and mysteriously
> intertwined, wing-beating creations:
> their hesitation and the suddenness of the heads
> and those strong leaves, whose sap

mounts like rage, finally spilling over
in a quick gesture that clenches
and thrusts itself out——:

Several of the *New Poems* participate even more directly
than this in the movements and energies they describe—the
chthonic windings of "The Tower" and the flamenco gestures
of "Spanish Dancer" are especially brilliant instances. Sel-
dom is visual perception an end in itself, and often it is the fo-
cus of a poem's deconstructive energies: a gazelle dissolves
into the stream of discontinuous metaphors that evoke it; a
marble fountain becomes a complex microcosm of fluid inter-
changes and secret relations. "As if"'s proliferate through the
poetry, keeping the reader's attention fixed not so much on the
object-world as on the zone where it and the imagination in-
teract. Even the icons of indifference that figure so promi-
nently in the *New Poems* live in the imagination whose desire
for relation they refuse:

> What do you know, stone creature, of our life?
> and is your face perhaps even more blissful
> when you hold your slate into the night?
> ("L'Ange du Méridien")

This interanimation of object and consciousness is, finally,
the great theme of the *New Poems*, in spite of their apparent
worship of states of withdrawal, apartness, and fulfilled iso-
lation. At their most radical they seek to open the dimensions
of what a phenomenologist like Merleau-Ponty would call the
"lived world," where subject and object are inseparable as-
pects of an imaginatively engendered unity. In "The Bowl of
Roses," the *New Poem* that goes furthest in this direction, what
begins as an object of perception is gradually transformed by
the imaginative impulse it releases into a multifarious world
teeming with metamorphic energies:

> What can't they be: was that yellow one,
> which lies there hollow and open, not the rind

of a fruit, in which the very same yellow,
more collected, orange-redder, was juice?
And was opening-out too much for this one,
since in the air its indescribable pink
took on the bitter aftertaste of violet?
And that cambric one, is it not a dress
in which, still soft and breath-warm, the chemise
clings, both of them cast off at once
in the morning shadows of the old forest pool?
And this one, opalescent porcelain,
fragile, a shallow china cup
and filled with tiny bright butterflies,—
and that one, which contains nothing but itself.

The transformative capacities of the roses are, of course,
those of the imagination that beholds them, but the effect is the
opposite of mere projection: the act of viewing seems rather
to cross over into a prior dimension where reality and imagi-
nation have yet to face each other off as opposites. Self-con-
tainment, arrived at from this direction, feels almost like the
opposite of itself, and triggers one of the great moments of
ontological redefinition in Rilke:

And aren't all that way, containing just themselves,
if self-containing means: to change the world outside
and wind and rain and patience of the spring
and guilt and restlessness and muffled fate
and the darkness of the evening earth
out to the changing and flying and fleeing of the clouds
and the vague influence of distant stars
into a hand full of inwardness.

Now it lies carefree in these open roses.

In a sense, the *New Poems* themselves are just such hands full
of inwardness. Open to the permeability of the inner and the
outer realms, their autonomy is that of things invested with a
new sense of self. They deny us subjectivity in order to restore
us to the world.

A word of explanation may be in order concerning the contents of this volume. Rilke originally published the *New Poems* in two successive, separately titled books: *New Poems (Neue Gedichte)* in December 1907, and *New Poems: The Other Part (Der Neuen Gedichte anderer Teil)* in July 1908. It was not until 1928, two years after his death, that they were brought together in a single volume. Both are intricately composed *books* of poetry, and even the most famous poems—"The Panther," for instance—take on a very different feel when read in context. But one can miss just as much by regarding the two books as simply Parts One and Two of a single work. For in spite of all the volumes have in common, they are distinct unities composed of different moods, personalities, and underlying architectures of theme and motif. They even mark different stages in Rilke's development, with the insistence on objective experience that enriches the lyric impulse of the first volume already in danger of hardening into something willed and brilliantly unfeeling in the second. We have everything to gain by bringing the separate unities of the two works back into focus. The poems included here under the title *New Poems* are accordingly those of the 1907 volume only; a translation of the 1908 poems will follow. It has seemed especially worth insisting on the integrity of the 1907 volume: its consistently high level of accomplishment and intricate structure of motif make it for me Rilke's greatest single achievement as a poet, as well as perhaps the happiest moment in his oeuvre. The last five poems in the volume have a cumulative impact that deserves the full weight of an ending: "The Bowl of Roses" is not a half-way point but a moment of visionary arrival.

I want to thank the National Endowment for the Humanities for a grant that made possible a year's worth of uninterrupted work on these translations. I would also like to thank Albert Cook, Richard Exner, John Felstiner, Philip Lopate, Scott McLean, Stephen Mitchell, and Leo Steinberg for their many valuable comments. I owe a special debt of gratitude to my colleague Michael Winkler, whose insights into Rilke and ear for poetic rhythms have proved invaluable resources; his patience and generosity have saved me countless embarrassments. And, finally, I am indebted to other translators of Rilke. I have tried to learn as much as I could from the daunting complete translations of the *New Poems* by J.B. Leishman, and from the *Selected Rilkes* of Stephen Mitchell, M.D. Herder Norton, C.F. MacIntyre, Robert Bly, Rika Lesser, and Franz Wright. For occasionally adopting a reading that a poem seemed absolutely to require, I beg forgiveness; I hope that whoever comes after me will find something worth taking from this volume.

E.S.

New Poems [1907]

Karl und Elisabeth von der Heydt
in Freundschaft

Früher Apollo

Wie manches Mal durch das noch unbelaubte
Gezweig ein Morgen durchsieht, der schon ganz
im Frühling ist: so ist in seinem Haupte
nichts was verhindern könnte, daß der Glanz

aller Gedichte uns fast tödlich träfe;
denn noch kein Schatten ist in seinem Schaun,
zu kühl für Lorbeer sind noch seine Schläfe
und später erst wird aus den Augenbraun

hochstämmig sich der Rosengarten heben,
aus welchem Blätter, einzeln, ausgelöst
hintreiben werden auf des Mundes Beben,

der jetzt noch still ist, niegebraucht und blinkend
und nur mit seinem Lächeln etwas trinkend
als würde ihm sein Singen eingeflößt.

Early Apollo

As sometimes between still leafless branches
a morning looks through that is already
radiant with spring: so nothing in his head
could obstruct the splendor of all poems

from striking us with almost lethal force;
for there is still no shadow in his gaze,
his temples are still too cool for laurel,
and only later from his eyebrows' arches

will the rose garden lift up tall-stemmed,
from which petals, one by one released
will drift down upon his mouth's trembling,

which now is still quiet, never-used, and gleaming
and only drinking something with its smile
as though its song were being infused in him.

Mädchen-Klage

Diese Neigung, in den Jahren,
da wir alle Kinder waren,
viel allein zu sein, war mild;
andern ging die Zeit im Streite,
und man hatte seine Seite,
seine Nähe, seine Weite,
einen Weg, ein Tier, ein Bild.

Und ich dachte noch, das Leben
hörte niemals auf zu geben,
daß man sich in sich besinnt.
Bin ich in mir nicht im Größten?
Will mich Meines nicht mehr trösten
und verstehen wie als Kind?

Plötzlich bin ich wie verstoßen,
und zu einem Übergroßen
wird mir diese Einsamkeit,
wenn, auf meiner Brüste Hügeln
stehend, mein Gefühl nach Flügeln
oder einem Ende schreit.

Girl's Lament

This inclination, in the years
when we were all children,
to be so much alone, was gentle;
for others time passed in fighting,
and one had one's faction,
one's near, one's far-off place,
a path, an animal, a picture.

And I still imagined that life
would never cease providing,
while one dwelt on things within.
Within myself am I not in this greatness?
Will what's mine no longer soothe
and understand me as when a child?

Suddenly I'm as if cast out,
and into something vast and ill-fitting
this solitude transforms,
when, standing on my breasts' hills,
my feeling screams for wings
or for an end.

Liebes-Lied

Wie soll ich meine Seele halten, daß
sie nicht an deine rührt? Wie soll ich sie
hinheben über dich zu andern Dingen?
Ach gerne möcht ich sie bei irgendwas
Verlorenem im Dunkel unterbringen
an einer fremden stillen Stelle, die
nicht weiterschwingt, wenn deine Tiefen schwingen.
Doch alles, was uns anrührt, dich und mich,
nimmt uns zusammen wie ein Bogenstrich,
der aus zwei Saiten *eine* Stimme zieht.
Auf welches Instrument sind wir gespannt?
Und welcher Geiger hat uns in der Hand?
O süßes Lied.

Love Song

How shall I keep my soul
from touching yours? How shall
I lift it over you toward other things?
Ah, I would like to lodge it
in the dark with some lost thing
on some foreign silent place
that doesn't tremble, when your depths stir.
Yet everything that touches *you* and *me*
takes us together like a bow's stroke
that from two strings draws *one* voice.
Across what instrument are we stretched taut?
And what player holds us in his hand?
O sweet song.

Eranna an Sappho

O du wilde weite Werferin:
Wie ein Speer bei andern Dingen
lag ich bei den Meinen. Dein Erklingen
warf mich weit. Ich weiß nicht *wo* ich bin.
Mich kann keiner wiederbringen.

Meine Schwestern denken mich und weben,
und das Haus ist voll vertrauter Schritte.
Ich allein bin fern und fortgegeben,
und ich zittere wie eine Bitte;
denn die schöne Göttin in der Mitte
ihrer Mythen glüht und lebt mein Leben.

Eranna to Sappho

O you fierce far-flinging hurler!
Like a spear among other things
I lay among my kin. Your music
launched me far. I don't know *where* I am.
No one can ever bring me back.

My sisters think of me and weave,
and the house is full of trusted footsteps.
I alone am distant and given over,
and I tremble like a plea;
for the lovely goddess burns in the middle
of her myths and lives my life.

Sappho an Eranna

Unruh will ich über dich bringen,
schwingen will ich dich, umrankter Stab.
Wie das Sterben will ich dich durchdringen
und dich weitergeben wie das Grab
an das Alles: allen diesen Dingen.

Sappho to Eranna

I want to flood you with unrest,
want to brandish you, you vine-clasped staff.
Like dying I want to pierce through you
and pass you on like the grave
to the All: to all these things.

Sappho an Alkaïos

Fragment

Und was hättest du mir denn zu sagen,
und was gehst du meine Seele an,
wenn sich deine Augen niederschlagen
vor dem nahen Nichtgesagten? Mann,

sieh, uns hat das Sagen dieser Dinge
hingerissen und bis in den Ruhm.
Wenn ich denke: unter euch verginge
dürftig unser süßes Mädchentum,

welches wir, ich Wissende und jene
mit mir Wissenden, vom Gott bewacht,
trugen unberührt, daß Mytilene
wie ein Apfelgarten in der Nacht
duftete vom Wachsen unsrer Brüste—.

Ja, auch dieser Brüste, die du nicht
wähltest wie zu Fruchtgewinden, Freier
mit dem weggesenkten Angesicht.
Geh und laß mich, daß zu meiner Leier
komme, was du abhältst: alles steht.

Dieser Gott ist nicht der Beistand Zweier,
aber wenn er durch den Einen geht
. . . .

Sappho to Alcaeus

Fragment

And what anyway could you have said to me,
and what concern has my soul for you,
if your eyes lower themselves timidly
when the not-said comes near? Man,

look, the saying of these things has
transported us, and even into fame.
When I think: beneath you our sweet
maidenhood would wretchedly perish,

which we, I who know and those who
know along with me, guarded by the god,
bore untouched, so that Mytilene
like an apple orchard in the night
grew fragrant with the swelling of our breasts.

Yes, these breasts too, which you did not select
as one intent on twining wreaths of fruit,
you suitor with the drooping face.
Go, leave me, that to my lyre may come
what you keep back: everything stands poised.

This god is no assistance to a pair,
but when he surges through the *one*

. . . .

The poem takes its cue from an exchange between Sappho and Alcaeus recorded by Aristotle in his *Rhetoric* (I.ix.20). Rilke paraphrases it in a letter of 25 July 1907 to his wife: "Alcaeus was a poet, who on an antique vase stands before Sappho with head lowered and lyre in hand, and one knows that he has said to her: 'Weaver of darkness, Sappho, you pure one with the honey-sweet smile, words throng to my lips, but a shame holds me back.' And she: 'Had you a wish in you for noble and beautiful things, and not base matters on your tongue, you would not have lowered your eyes in shame and would have rightly spoken.'" Rilke's Sappho (a forthright sensualist) seems to pick up where Aristotle's leaves off.

Grabmal eines jungen Mädchens

Wir gedenkens noch. Das ist, als müßte
alles dieses einmal wieder sein.
Wie ein Baum an der Limonenküste
trugst du deine kleinen leichten Brüste
in das Rauschen seines Bluts hinein:

—jenes Gottes.
                    Und es war der schlanke
Flüchtling, der Verwöhnende der Fraun.
Süß und glühend, warm wie dein Gedanke,
überschattend deine frühe Flanke
und geneigt wie deine Augenbraun.

Funeral Monument of a Young Girl

We still remember. It is as if
all this must once again exist.
Like a tree along the southern coast
you bore your small light breasts
out into the surging of his blood:

—that god's.
         And it was the slender
fugitive, that pamperer of women.
Sweet and glowing, warm like your thought,
overshadowing your young flanks
and arched the way your eyebrows were.

Opfer

O wie blüht mein Leib aus jeder Ader
duftender, seitdem ich dich erkenn;
sieh, ich gehe schlanker und gerader,
und du wartest nur—: wer bist du denn?

Sieh: ich fühle, wie ich mich entferne,
wie ich Altes, Blatt um Blatt, verlier.
Nur dein Lächeln steht wie lauter Sterne
über dir und bald auch über mir.

Alles was durch meine Kinderjahre
namenlos noch und wie Wasser glänzt,
will ich nach dir nennen am Altare,
der entzündet ist von deinem Haare
und mit deinen Brüsten leicht bekränzt.

Sacrifice

How my body blooms from every vein
more fragrantly, since I first knew you;
look, I walk slimmer and straighter,
and you only wait—: who are you then?

Look: I feel how I'm moving away,
How I'm shedding my old life, leaf by leaf.
Only your smile stands like pure stars
over you and, soon now, over me.

Everything that shines through my childhood years
still nameless and gleaming like water,
I will name after you at the altar,
which your hair has set on fire
and your breasts have gently wreathed.

Östliches Taglied

Ist dieses Bette nicht wie eine Küste,
ein Küstenstreifen nur, darauf wir liegen?
Nichts ist gewiß als deine hohen Brüste,
die mein Gefühl in Schwindeln überstiegen.

Denn diese Nacht, in der so vieles schrie,
in der sich Tiere rufen und zerreißen,
ist sie uns nicht entsetzlich fremd? Und wie:
was draußen langsam anhebt, Tag geheißen,
ist das uns denn verständlicher als sie?

Man müßte so sich ineinanderlegen
wie Blütenblätter um die Staubgefäße:
so sehr ist überall das Ungemäße
und häuft sich an und stürzt sich uns entgegen.

Doch während wir uns aneinander drücken,
um nicht zu sehen, wie es ringsum naht,
kann es aus dir, kann es aus mir sich zücken:
denn unsre Seelen leben von Verrat.

Eastern Aubade

Is this bed not like some coast,
just a strip of coast on which we lie?
Nothing is certain except your high breasts,
which mounted dizzily beyond my feeling.

For this night, in which so many things screamed,
in which beasts call and tear each other,
does its strangeness not appall us? And yet:
what outside slowly dawns, called day,
do we find it any more familiar?

One would have to lie as tightly intertwined
as flower petals around the stamen:
for the unrestrained stands everywhere
and masses and plunges toward us.

Yet while we press against each other,
in order not to see it closing in,
can it draw itself from you, from me:
for our souls live on treason.

Abisag

Sie lag. Und ihre Kinderarme waren
von Dienern um den Welkenden gebunden,
auf dem sie lag die süßen langen Stunden,
ein wenig bang vor seinen vielen Jahren.

Und manchmal wandte sie in seinem Barte
ihr Angesicht, wenn eine Eule schrie;
und alles, was die Nacht war, kam und scharte
mit Bangen und Verlangen sich um sie.

Die Sterne zitterten wie ihresgleichen,
ein Duft ging suchend durch das Schlafgemach,
der Vorhang rührte sich und gab ein Zeichen,
und leise ging ihr Blick dem Zeichen nach—.

Aber sie hielt sich an dem dunkeln Alten
und, von der Nacht der Nächte nicht erreicht,
lag sie auf seinem fürstlichen Erkalten
jungfräulich und wie eine Seele leicht.

Abishag

She lay. And her child's arms were tied
by maidservants around the fading king,
on whom she lay through the sweet slow hours,
a little frightened of his many years.

And now and then she turned her face
in his beard, whenever an owl screamed;
and everything that the night was came and
flocked with fear and desire around her.

The stars trembled just as she did,
a scent went searching through the sleeping room,
the curtain stirred and gave a sign,
and her gaze softly followed after it—.

But she held on to the obscure old man
and, beyond the Night of Nights' dark reach,
lay on his potency's increasing coldness
virginally, and lightly like a soul.

Kings I:1-4: "And when the king was old and burdened with years, he could
not grow warm, even though they covered him with clothes. Then his ser-
vants said to him: 'Let there be sought for my lord the king a young girl, a vir-
gin, who will stand before the king and care for him and sleep in his arms and
warm my lord the king.' And they searched for a beautiful girl throughout all
the lands of Israel, and found Abishag from Shunam, and brought her to the
king. And she was indeed beautiful, and she cared for the king and served him.
But the king knew her not."

Der König saß und sann den leeren Tag
getaner Taten, ungefühlter Lüste
und seiner Lieblingshündin, der er pflag—.
Aber am Abend wölbte Abisag
sich über ihm. Sein wirres Leben lag
verlassen wie verrufne Meeresküste
unter dem Sternbild ihrer stillen Brüste.

Und manchmal, als ein Kundiger der Frauen,
erkannte er durch seine Augenbrauen
den unbewegten, küsselosen Mund;
und sah: ihres Gefühles grüne Rute
neigte sich nicht herab zu seinem Grund.
Ihn fröstelte. Er horchte wie ein Hund
und suchte sich in seinem letzten Blute.

II

The king sat thinking through the empty day
of deeds accomplished, of unfelt pleasures,
and of his favorite dog, on whom he doted.
But in the evening Abishag arched
over him. His tangled life lay
abandoned like an ill-famed coast
beneath the constellation of her silent breasts.

And now and then, as one adept in women,
he recognized through his eyebrows
the unmoved, kissless mouth;
and saw: her feeling's green divining rod
did not point downward to his depths.
A chill went through him. He hearkened like a hound
and sought himself in his last blood.

David singt vor Saul

I

König, hörst du, wie mein Saitenspiel
Fernen wirft, durch die wir uns bewegen:
Sterne treiben uns verwirrt entgegen,
und wir fallen endlich wie ein Regen,
und es blüht, wo dieser Regen fiel.

Mädchen blühen, die du noch erkannt,
die jetzt Frauen sind und mich verführen;
den Geruch der Jungfraun kannst du spüren,
und die Knaben stehen, angespannt
schlank und atmend, an verschwiegnen Türen.

Daß mein Klang dir alles wiederbrächte.
Aber trunken taumelt mein Getön:
Deine Nächte, König, deine Nächte—,
und wie waren, die dein Schaffen schwächte,
o wie waren alle Leiber schön.

Dein Erinnern glaub ich zu begleiten,
weil ich ahne. Doch auf welchen Saiten
greif ich dir ihr dunkles Lustgestöhn?—

David Sings before Saul

I

King, do you hear how my lyre's play
casts distances, through which we move?
Stars drift up to us bewildered,
and we fall at long last like a rain,
and it flowers where that rain came down.

Girls flower, whom back then you knew,
who now are women and tempt me;
you can detect the scent of virgins,
and young boys stand, tensed
slim and breathing, at concealed doors.

That my sound could bring it back to you!
But my music staggers drunkenly:
Your nights, King, your nights—,
and how lovely, weakened by your prowess,
O how lovely all those bodies were.

Your remembering I can accompany,
since I can see it. But on what strings
might I pluck for you their dark moans of pleasure?

König, der du alles dieses hattest
und der du mit lauter Leben mich
überwältigest und überschattest:
komm aus deinem Throne und zerbrich
meine Harfe, die du so ermattest.

Sie ist wie ein abgenommner Baum:
durch die Zweige, die dir Frucht getragen,
schaut jetzt eine Tiefe wie von Tagen
welche kommen—, und ich kenn sie kaum.

Laß mich nicht mehr bei der Harfe schlafen;
sieh dir diese Knabenhand da an:
glaubst du, König, daß sie die Oktaven
eines Leibes noch nicht greifen kann?

II

King, you who had all this
and who with sheer life
overwhelm and overshadow me:
come down from your throne and smash
my harp, which you so exhaust.

It is like a tree picked bare:
through the branches that bore you fruit
a depth now gazes, as of days
that approach—; and I scarcely know them.

Let me sleep no longer beside the harp;
take a look at this boyish hand:
do you think, King, that it still can't
span the octaves of a body?

III

König, birgst du dich in Finsternissen,
und ich hab dich doch in der Gewalt.
Sieh, mein festes Lied ist nicht gerissen,
und der Raum wird um uns beide kalt.
Mein verwaistes Herz und dein verworrnes
hängen in den Wolken deines Zornes,
wütend ineinander eingebissen
und zu einem einzigen verkrallt.

Fühlst du jetzt, wie wir uns umgestalten?
König, König, das Gewicht wird Geist.
Wenn wir uns nur aneinander halten,
du am Jungen, König, ich am Alten,
sind wir fast wie ein Gestirn das kreist.

III

King, you hide yourself in darknesses,
and still I have you in control.
Look, my sturdy song has not been torn,
and space grows cold around us both.
My orphaned heart and your confounded one
hang in the storm-clouds of your anger,
furiously bitten into one another
and clawed together toward a single thing.

Can you feel, now, how we reconfigure?
King, King, heaviness becomes spirit.
If only we hold on to one another,
you to youth, King, I to age,
we are almost like a star that circles.

Josuas Landtag

So wie der Strom am Ausgang seine Dämme
durchbricht mit seiner Mündung Übermaß,
so brach nun durch die Ältesten der Stämme
zum letzten Mal die Stimme Josuas.

Wie waren die geschlagen, welche lachten,
wie hielten alle Herz und Hände an,
als hübe sich der Lärm von dreißig Schlachten
in einem Mund; und dieser Mund begann.

Und wieder waren Tausende voll Staunen
wie an dem großen Tag vor Jericho,
nun aber waren in ihm die Posaunen,
und ihres Lebens Mauern schwankten so,

daß sie sich wälzten von Entsetzen trächtig
und wehrlos schon und überwältigt, eh
sie's noch gedachten, wie er eigenmächtig
zu Gibeon die Sonne anschrie: steh:

Und Gott ging hin, erschrocken wie ein Knecht,
und hielt die Sonne, bis ihm seine Hände
wehtaten, ob dem schlachtenden Geschlecht,
nur weil da einer wollte, daß sie stände.

Und das war dieser; dieser Alte wars,
von dem sie meinten, daß er nicht mehr gelte
inmitten seines hundertzehnten Jahrs.
Da stand er auf und brach in ihre Zelte.

Er ging wie Hagel nieder über Halmen:
Was wollt ihr Gott versprechen? Ungezählt

Joshua's Council

As the river at its outlet breaks through
its dams with its mouth's accumulations,
so now for the last time the voice of Joshua
broke through the elders of the tribes.

How those were smitten, who were laughing,
how all hearts and hands were halted,
as though the din from thirty battles rose
in one mouth; and that mouth began.

And again thousands were lost in wonder
as on that great day in front of Jericho,
only now the trumpets were inside him
and their own lives' walls were swaying so

that they were writhing in throes of horror
and helpless already and overwhelmed
before they thought back to how high-handedly
he shouted to the sun in Gideon: stand:

And God went off, cowering like a serf,
and held the sun above that murdering
race until his hands ached, just because
one man willed that it should stand.

And this was that man; this old patriarch
whose voice they thought had lost all force
in the middle of his hundred-tenth year.
Then he stood up and broke into their tents.

He descended like hail upon stalks of corn:
What would you promise God? Uncounted

stehn um euch Götter, wartend daß ihr wählt.
Doch wenn ihr wählt, wird euch der Herr zermalmen.

Und dann, mit einem Hochmut ohnegleichen:
Ich und mein Haus, wir bleiben ihm vermählt.

Da schrien sie alle: Hilf uns, gieb ein Zeichen
und stärke uns zu unserer schweren Wahl.

Aber sie sahn ihn, wie seit Jahren schweigend,
zu seiner festen Stadt am Berge steigend;
und dann nicht mehr. Es war das letzte Mal.

gods stand around you, waiting on your choice.
Yet when you choose, the Lord will crush you.

And then, with peerless arrogance:
I and my house are still his bride.

At that they all cried: Help us, give a sign
and strengthen us for our hard choice.

But they saw him, as if silent for years,
ascending to his mountain stronghold;
and then no more. It was the last time.

Der Auszug des verlorenen Sohnes

Nun fortzugehn von alledem Verworrnen,
das unser ist und uns doch nicht gehört,
das, wie das Wasser in den alten Bornen,
uns zitternd spiegelt und das Bild zerstört;
von allem diesen, das sich wie mit Dornen
noch einmal an uns anhängt—fortzugehn
und Das und Den,
die man schon nicht mehr sah
(so täglich waren sie und so gewöhnlich),
auf einmal anzuschauen: sanft, versöhnlich
und wie an einem Anfang und von nah;
und ahnend einzusehn, wie unpersönlich,
wie über alle hin das Leid geschah,
von dem die Kindheit voll war bis zum Rand—:
Und dann doch fortzugehen, Hand aus Hand,
als ob man ein Geheiltes neu zerrisse,
und fortzugehn: wohin? Ins Ungewisse,
weit in ein unverwandtes warmes Land,
das hinter allem Handeln wie Kulisse
gleichgültig sein wird: Garten oder Wand;
und fortzugehn: warum? Aus Drang, aus Artung,
aus Ungeduld, aus dunkler Erwartung,
aus Unverständlichkeit und Unverstand:

Dies alles auf sich nehmen und vergebens
vielleicht Gehaltnes fallen lassen, um
allein zu sterben, wissend nicht warum—

Ist das der Eingang eines neuen Lebens?

The Departure of the Prodigal Son

Now to go away from all this tangledness
that is ours and yet does not belong to us,
that like the water in the old wells
mirrors us trembling and destroys the image;
from all of this, which as if with thorns
once more clings to us—to go away
and at *this* and *that*,
which already you no longer saw
(they were so everyday and so commonplace),
suddenly to look: gently, contritely,
and as if in a beginning and from up close;
and to fathom how impersonally,
how over everyone the misery swept
that filled childhood up to the brim—:
And then still to go away, hand from hand,
as if you ripped a new-healed wound,
and to go away: where? Into uncertainty,
far into some unrelated warm land
that behind all action like a backdrop
will be indifferent: garden or wall;
and to go away: why? From urge, from instinct,
from impatience, from dark expectation,
from not understanding and not being understood:

To take all this on yourself and in vain
perhaps let fall things tightly held,
in order to die alone, not knowing why—

Is this the entrance to a new life?

Der Ölbaum-Garten

Er ging hinauf unter dem grauen Laub
ganz grau und aufgelöst im Ölgelände
und legte seine Stirne voller Staub
tief in das Staubigsein der heißen Hände.

Nach allem dies. Und dieses war der Schluß.
Jetzt soll ich gehen, während ich erblinde,
und warum willst Du, daß ich sagen muß
Du seist, wenn ich Dich selber nicht mehr finde.

Ich finde Dich nicht mehr. Nicht in mir, nein.
Nicht in den andern. Nicht in diesem Stein.
Ich finde Dich nicht mehr. Ich bin allein.

Ich bin allein mit aller Menschen Gram,
den ich durch Dich zu lindern unternahm,
der Du nicht bist. O namenlose Scham...

Später erzählte man: ein Engel kam—.

Warum ein Engel? Ach es kam die Nacht
und blätterte gleichgültig in den Bäumen.
Die Jünger rührten sich in ihren Träumen.
Warum ein Engel? Ach es kam die Nacht.

Die Nacht, die kam, war keine ungemeine;
so gehen hunderte vorbei.
Da schlafen Hunde und da liegen Steine.
Ach eine traurige, ach irgendeine,
die wartet, bis es wieder Morgen sei.

Denn Engel kommen nicht zu solchen Betern,
und Nächte werden nicht um solche groß.

The Olive Garden

He went up under the gray leaves
all gray and dissolved in olive country
and laid his forehead full of dust
deep in the dustiness of burning hands.

After everything this. And this was the end.
Now I am to go, while I grow blind,
and why is it Your will that I must say
You are, when I myself no longer find You.

I find You no longer. Not in me.
Not in the others. Not in this stone.
I find You no longer. I am aloné.

I am alone with all of human grief,
which through You I undertook to lighten,
You who are not. O ineffable shame . . .

Later they would say: an angel came—.

Why an angel? Ah, what came was night,
and leafed indifferently in the trees.
The disciples stirred in their dreams.
Why an angel? Ah, what came was night.

The night that came was nothing special;
hundreds go by just that way.
Dogs sleep in them, stones lie in them.
A sad night, ah any night at all
that waits until it's once more morning.

For angels don't come to the prayers of such men,
and nights don't grow large around them.

Die Sich-Verlierenden läßt alles los,
und sie sind preisgegeben von den Vätern
und ausgeschlossen aus der Mütter Schooß.

The self-losing are let go by everything,
and they are abandoned by their fathers
and locked out of their mothers' wombs.

Pietà

So seh ich, Jesus, deine Füße wieder,
die damals eines Jünglings Füße waren,
da ich sie bang entkleidete und wusch;
wie standen sie verwirrt in meinen Haaren
und wie ein weißes Wild im Dornenbusch.

So seh ich deine niegeliebten Glieder
zum erstenmal in dieser Liebesnacht.
Wir legten uns noch nie zusammen nieder,
und nun wird nur bewundert und gewacht.

Doch, siehe, deine Hände sind zerrissen—:
Geliebter, nicht von mir, von meinen Bissen.
Dein Herz steht offen und man kann hinein:
das hätte dürfen nur mein Eingang sein.

Nun bist du müde, und dein müder Mund
hat keine Lust zu meinem wehen Munde—.
O Jesus, Jesus, wann war unsre Stunde?
Wie gehn wir beide wunderlich zugrund.

Pietà

So like this, Jesus, I see your feet again
that were a young man's feet that time
I fearfully unshod and washed them:
how they stood all tangled in my hair
and like a white stag in a thornbush.

So like this I see your never-cherished limbs
for the first time in this night of love.
Never yet have we lain down together,
and now there's only awe and keeping watch.

But look, your hands are torn—:
Dearest, not from me, not from my biting.
Your heart stands open and anyone may enter:
it should have been a way in kept for me.

Now you are tired, and your weary lips
have no desire for my aching mouth—.
O Jesus, Jesus, when was our hour?
How strangely both of us are perishing.

Gesang der Frauen an den Dichter

Sieh, wie sich alles auftut: so sind wir;
denn wir sind nichts als solche Seligkeit.
Was Blut und Dunkel war in einem Tier,
das wuchs in uns zur Seele an und schreit

als Seele weiter. Und es schreit nach dir.
Du freilich nimmst es nur in dein Gesicht
als sei es Landschaft: sanft und ohne Gier.
Und darum meinen wir, du bist es nicht,

nach dem es schreit. Und doch, bist du nicht der,
an den wir uns ganz ohne Rest verlören?
Und werden wir in irgend einem *mehr?*

Mit uns geht das Unendliche *vorbei.*
Du aber sei, du Mund, daß wir es hören,
du aber, du Uns-Sagender: du sei.

Song of the Women to the Poet

Look, how everything unfolds: we're that way;
for we are nothing but such bliss.
What was blood and darkness in an animal
grew on in us to soul and continues

to scream out as soul. And it screams for you.
You it's true take it only into your face
as if it were landscape: gently and without craving.
And therefore we suppose it isn't you

for which it screams. And yet, are you not he
on whom we lose ourselves without reserve?
And do we become in any person *more*?

With us the infinite goes *past*.
But you be, you mouth, that we may hear it,
but you, you sayer of us: you be.

Der Tod des Dichters

Er lag. Sein aufgestelltes Antlitz war
bleich und verweigernd in den steilen Kissen,
seitdem die Welt und dieses von-ihr-Wissen,
von seinen Sinnen abgerissen,
zurückfiel an das teilnahmslose Jahr.

Die, so ihn leben sahen, wußten nicht,
wie sehr er Eines war mit allem diesen;
denn Dieses: diese Tiefen, diese Wiesen
und diese Wasser *waren* sein Gesicht.

O sein Gesicht war diese ganze Weite,
die jetzt noch zu ihm will und um ihn wirbt;
und seine Maske, die nun bang verstirbt,
ist zart und offen wie die Innenseite
von einer Frucht, die an der Luft verdirbt.

The Poet's Death

He lay. His erected countenance was
pale and refusing in the steep pillows,
now that the world and this knowledge
of it, ripped away from his senses,
had fallen back to the indifferent year.

Those who saw him living didn't know
how completely one he was with all of this;
for this: these meadows, these valleys
and these waters *were* his face.

O his face was this entire expanse,
that now still seeks him and tries to woo him;
and his mask, which now fearfully dies,
is tender and open, like the inside
of a piece of fruit that spoils in the air.

Buddha

Als ob er horchte. Stille: eine Ferne ...
Wir halten ein und hören sie nicht mehr.
Und er ist Stern. Und andre große Sterne,
die wir nicht sehen, stehen um ihn her.

O er ist Alles. Wirklich, warten wir,
daß er uns sähe? Sollte er bedürfen?
Und wenn wir hier uns vor ihm niederwürfen,
er bliebe tief und träge wie ein Tier.

Denn das, was uns zu seinen Füßen reißt,
das kreist in ihm seit Millionen Jahren.
Er, der vergißt was wir erfahren
und der erfährt was uns verweist.

Buddha

As if he listened. Stillness: something distant . . .
we check ourselves and cease to hear it.
And he is Star. And other giant stars
we do not see stand far around him.

O he is everything. Do we really wait
in hope he'll see us? What might he need?
Even if we threw ourselves down before him,
he'd remain deep and idle like a beast.

For what tears us roughly to his feet
has circled in him for a million years.
He, who forgets what we experience
and who experiences what casts us out.

L'Ange du Méridien

Chartres

Im Sturm, der um die starke Kathedrale
wie ein Verneiner stürzt der denkt und denkt,
fühlt man sich zärtlicher mit einem Male
von deinem Lächeln zu dir hingelenkt:

lächelnder Engel, fühlende Figur,
mit einem Mund, gemacht aus hundert Munden:
gewahrst du gar nicht, wie dir unsre Stunden
abgleiten von der vollen Sonnenuhr,

auf der des Tages ganze Zahl zugleich,
gleich wirklich, steht in tiefem Gleichgewichte,
als wären alle Stunden reif und reich.

Was weißt du, Steinerner, von unserm Sein?
und hältst du mit noch seligerm Gesichte
vielleicht die Tafel in die Nacht hinein?

L'Ange du Méridien

Chartres

In the storm that swirls around the strong cathedral
like some nay-sayer who thinks and thinks,
all at once one feels more tenderly
guided to you by your smile:

smiling angel, feeling figure,
with a mouth made from a hundred mouths:
do you not become at all aware
of how our hours slip off your full sundial,

on which the day's whole sum at once,
in equal force, stands in deep balance,
as if all hours were ripe and rich.

What do you know, stone creature, of our life?
and is your face perhaps even more blissful
when you hold your slate into the night?

The poem describes the "Angel with the Sundial" on the facade of the
Chartres cathedral. The name Rilke gives it in the poem's title is not the one it
is commonly known by, and seems a deliberate thematic gesture on his part.
The statue's common French designation is "L'Ange au cadran solaire"; Ro-
din refers to it throughout his book on French cathedrals as "L'Ange de
Chartres" or simply "L'Ange," and Rilke himself describes it in a letter of 26
January 1906 to his wife as merely "a slim weatherbeaten angel which holds
a sundial out in front of it."

Die Kathedrale

In jenen kleinen Städten, wo herum
die alten Häuser wie ein Jahrmarkt hocken,
der *sie* bemerkt hat plötzlich und, erschrocken,
die Buden zumacht und, ganz zu und stumm,

die Schreier still, die Trommeln angehalten,
zu ihr hinaufhorcht aufgeregten Ohrs—:
dieweil sie ruhig immer in dem alten
Faltenmantel ihrer Contreforts
dasteht und von den Häusern gar nicht weiß:

in jenen kleinen Städten kannst du sehn,
wie sehr entwachsen ihrem Umgangskreis
die Kathedralen waren. Ihr Erstehn
ging über alles fort, so wie den Blick
des eignen Lebens viel zu große Nähe
fortwährend übersteigt, und als geschähe
nichts anderes; als wäre Das Geschick,
was sich in ihnen aufhäuft ohne Maßen,
versteinert und zum Dauernden bestimmt,
nicht Das, was unten in den dunkeln Straßen
vom Zufall irgendwelche Namen nimmt
und darin geht, wie Kinder Grün und Rot
und was der Krämer hat als Schürze tragen.
Da war Geburt in diesen Unterlagen,
und Kraft und Andrang war in diesem Ragen
und Liebe überall wie Wein und Brot,
und die Portale voller Liebesklagen.
Das Leben zögerte im Stundenschlagen,
und in den Türmen, welche voll Entsagen
auf einmal nicht mehr stiegen, war der Tod.

The Cathedral

In those small cities, where the houses
squat all around like a crowded fair
that has suddenly noticed *it*, and, startled,
shuts up its stalls, and, stock-still and speechless,

its barkers hushed, its drums halted,
strains up toward it excited ears—:
while it stands there calmly in the same
old pleated mantle of its contreforts
and knows nothing whatever of the houses:

in those small cities you can see
by how far the cathedrals had outgrown
their circle of relations. Their arising
went on over everything, just as our own
life's too close proximity constantly
surmounts our view, and as if nothing else
took place; as if destining were
what heaps up in them without measure,
transformed to stone and meant for enduring,
not what down below in the dark streets
takes from chance any random name
and goes along in it, the way children
wear green and red and what the shop has in aprons.
There was birth in all this groundwork,
and strength and surge was in this towering,
and love everywhere like wine and bread,
and the portals filled with love's laments.
Life hesitated in the hours' tolling,
and in the spires, which anxious to renounce
suddenly ceased rising, there was Death.

Das Portal

I
Da blieben sie, als wäre jene Flut
zurückgetreten, deren großes Branden
an diesen Steinen wusch, bis sie entstanden;
sie nahm im Fallen manches Attribut

aus ihren Händen, welche viel zu gut
und gebend sind, um etwas festzuhalten.
Sie blieben, von den Formen in Basalten
durch einen Nimbus, einen Bischofshut,

bisweilen durch ein Lächeln unterschieden,
für das ein Antlitz seiner Stunden Frieden
bewahrt hat als ein stilles Zifferblatt;

jetzt fortgerückt ins Leere ihres Tores,
waren sie einst die Muschel eines Ohres
und fingen jedes Stöhnen dieser Stadt.

The Portal

I
They endured here, as if that flood-tide
had subsided, whose great breakers
washed upon these stones till they emerged;
it took in its ebb many an attribute

from their hands, which are much too good
and giving to hold something tightly.
They endured, distinguished from the forms
in basalt by a nimbus, a bishop's hat,

occasionally by a smile, for which
a countenance has protected its hours'
harmony like a silent clock-face;

now drawn back rapt into the emptiness
of its door, it was once the conch of an ear
and caught this city's every groaning.

Sehr viele Weite ist gemeint damit:
so wie mit den Kulissen einer Szene
die Welt gemeint ist; und so wie durch jene
der Held im Mantel seiner Handlung tritt:—

so tritt das Dunkel dieses Tores handelnd
auf seiner Tiefe tragisches Theater,
so grenzenlos und wallend wie Gott-Vater
und so wie Er sich wunderlich verwandelnd

in einen Sohn, der aufgeteilt ist hier
auf viele kleine beinah stumme Rollen,
genommen aus des Elends Zubehör.

Denn nur noch so entsteht (das wissen wir)
aus Blinden, Fortgeworfenen und Tollen
der Heiland wie ein einziger Akteur.

II
So much distance is meant by it:
just as with the backdrop of a scene
the world is meant; and as through that scene
the hero strides, cloaked in his action's mantle:—

so the darkness of this doorway strides acting
onto the tragic theater of its depths,
as boundless and seething as God the Father
and just as He transforming wondrously

into a Son, who is distributed here
among many small, almost unspeaking roles,
all taken from misery's repertoire.

For it's only (this we know) from
the blind, the cast-out, and the mad
that, like a great actor, the Saviour emerges.

III

So ragen sie, die Herzen angehalten
(sie stehn auf Ewigkeit und gingen nie);
nur selten tritt aus dem Gefäll der Falten
eine Gebärde, aufrecht, steil wie sie,

und bleibt nach einem halben Schritte stehn
wo die Jahrhunderte sie überholen.
Sie sind im Gleichgewicht auf den Konsolen,
in denen eine Welt, die sie nicht sehn,

die Welt der Wirrnis, die sie nicht zertraten,
Figur und Tier, wie um sie zu gefährden,
sich krümmt und schüttelt und sie dennoch hält:

weil die Gestalten dort wie Akrobaten
sich nur so zuckend und so wild gebärden,
damit der Stab auf ihrer Stirn nicht fällt.

III

They tower thus, their hearts held in
(they stand on eternity and never walked);
only rarely from the fall of the folds
a gesture steps, erect, steep as they are,

and after a half-stride remains standing
where the centuries overtake it.
They are in equilibrium on the consoles
in which a world they do not see,

the world of turmoil, which they didn't crush,
figure and beast, as if to imperil them,
bends and shakes and nevertheless holds them:

since the forms there like acrobats
only keep twisting and jerking so wildly,
so that the staffs on their foreheads don't fall.

Die Fensterrose

Da drin: das träge Treten ihrer Tatzen
macht eine Stille, die dich fast verwirrt;
und wie dann plötzlich eine von den Katzen
den Blick an ihr, der hin und wieder irrt,

gewaltsam in ihr großes Auge nimmt,—
den Blick, der, wie von eines Wirbels Kreis
ergriffen, eine kleine Weile schwimmt
und dann versinkt und nichts mehr von sich weiß,

wenn dieses Auge, welches scheinbar ruht,
sich auftut und zusammenschlägt mit Tosen
und ihn hineinreißt bis ins rote Blut—:

So griffen einstmals aus dem Dunkelsein
der Kathedralen große Fensterrosen
ein Herz und rissen es in Gott hinein.

The Rose Window

In there: the lazy pacing of their paws
creates a stillness that's almost dizzying;
and how, then, suddenly one of the cats
takes the gaze on it, that strays now and then,

violently into its great eye,—
the gaze that, as if seized by a whirlpool's
circle, for a little while swims
and then sinks and ceases to remember,

when this eye, which apparently rests,
opens and slams shut with a roaring
and tears it deep into the red blood—:

Thus, long ago, out of the darkness
the cathedrals' great rose windows
seized a heart and tore it into God.

Das Kapitäl

Wie sich aus eines Traumes Ausgeburten
aufsteigend aus verwirrendem Gequäl
der nächste Tag erhebt: so gehn die Gurten
der Wölbung aus dem wirren Kapitäl

und lassen drin, gedrängt und rätselhaft
verschlungen, flügelschlagende Geschöpfe:
ihr Zögern und das Plötzliche der Köpfe
und jene starken Blätter, deren Saft

wie Jähzorn steigt, sich schließlich überschlagend
in einer schnellen Geste, die sich ballt
und sich heraushält—: alles aufwärtsjagend,

was immer wieder mit dem Dunkel kalt
herunterfällt, wie Regen Sorge tragend
für dieses alten Wachstums Unterhalt.

The Capital

As out of a dream's monstrous engenderings
climbing up out of entangling anguish
the next day rises: so the vaulting's ribs
arch out of the tangled capital

and leave there, crowded and mysteriously
intertwined, wing-beating creations:
their hesitation and the suddenness of the heads
and those strong leaves, whose sap

mounts like rage, finally spilling over
in a quick gesture that clenches
and thrusts itself out—: everything chasing upward

what always with the darkness coldly
falls down again, like rain bearing care
for this old growth's subsistence.

Gott im Mittelalter

Und sie hatten Ihn in sich erspart
und sie wollten, daß er sei und richte,
und sie hängten schließlich wie Gewichte
(zu verhindern seine Himmelfahrt)

an ihn ihrer großen Kathedralen
Last und Masse. Und er sollte nur
über seine grenzenlosen Zahlen
zeigend kreisen und wie eine Uhr

Zeichen geben ihrem Tun und Tagwerk.
Aber plötzlich kam er ganz in Gang,
und die Leute der entsetzten Stadt

ließen ihn, vor seiner Stimme bang,
weitergehn mit ausgehängtem Schlagwerk
und entflohn vor seinem Zifferblatt.

God in the Middle Ages

And they'd saved Him up inside themselves
and they wanted him to be and judge,
and finally (to keep him from ascending)
they attached to him like weight

their great cathedrals' bulk and burden.
And all he was supposed to do
was over all his boundless numbers
circle pointing, and like a clock give signs

to guide their day-to-day transactions.
But suddenly he got all the way in gear,
and the people of the horrified city

allowed him, frightened of his voice,
to go on with striking-works yanked out,
and fled before his silent dial-face.

Morgue

Da liegen sie bereit, als ob es gälte,
nachträglich eine Handlung zu erfinden,
die mit einander und mit dieser Kälte
sie zu versöhnen weiß und zu verbinden;

denn das ist alles noch wie ohne Schluß.
Wasfür ein Name hätte in den Taschen
sich finden sollen? An dem Überdruß
um ihren Mund hat man herumgewaschen:

er ging nicht ab; er wurde nur ganz rein.
Die Bärte stehen, noch ein wenig härter,
doch ordentlicher im Geschmack der Wärter,

nur um die Gaffenden nicht anzuwidern.
Die Augen haben hinter ihren Lidern
sich umgewandt und schauen jetzt hinein.

Morgue

They lie here ready, as if some action
would have to be made up belatedly
whose force could reconcile and bind them
with one another and with this cold;

for it all still seems to lack conclusion.
What sort of name might have turned up
inside the pockets? All about the boredom
around their mouths someone has washed:

it didn't come off; it just became quite clean.
Their beards stand, only a little stiffer,
but tidier, to the attendant's taste,

so that those gawking won't be repulsed.
The eyes have turned around behind their lids
and fix their gaze now on what's within.

Der Gefangene

I
Meine Hand hat nur noch eine
Gebärde, mit der sie verscheucht;
auf die alten Steine
fällt es aus Felsen feucht.

Ich höre nur dieses Klopfen
und mein Herz hält Schritt
mit dem Gehen der Tropfen
und vergeht damit.

Tropften sie doch schneller,
käme doch wieder ein Tier.
Irgendwo war es heller—.
Aber was wissen wir.

The Prisoner

I
My hand has only one gesture
left, with which it frightens off;
on the old stones wetness
falls from rock.

I hear only this knocking
and my heart keeps pace
with the passing of the drops
and fades off with it.

If only they'd drop faster,
if an animal came again.
Somewhere it was brighter—.
But what do we know.

II

Denk dir, das was jetzt Himmel ist und Wind,
Luft deinem Mund und deinem Auge Helle,
das würde Stein bis um die kleine Stelle
an der dein Herz und deine Hände sind.

Und was jetzt in dir morgen heißt und: dann
und: späterhin und nächstes Jahr und weiter—
das würde wund in dir und voller Eiter
und schwäre nur und bräche nicht mehr an.

Und das was war, das wäre irre und
raste in dir herum, den lieben Mund
der niemals lachte, schäumend von Gelächter.

Und das was Gott war, wäre nur dein Wächter
und stopfte boshaft in das letzte Loch
ein schmutziges Auge. Und du lebtest doch.

II

Imagine that what now is sky and wind,
air for your mouth and brightness for your eyes,
that became stone right up to the small place
where your heart and your hands are.

And what now in you is "tomorrow" and "then"
and "later on" and "next year" and "after that"—
that became galled in you and full of pus
and only festered and no longer broke.

And that which was, were now insane and
raged about in you, your kindly mouth
that never laughed, foaming with laughter.

And that which God was, were just your watcher
and crammed maliciously in the last hole
a filthy eye. And yet you lived.

Der Panther

Im Jardin des Plantes, Paris

Sein Blick ist vom Vorübergehn der Stäbe
so müd geworden, daß er nichts mehr hält.
Ihm ist, als ob es tausend Stäbe gäbe
und hinter tausend Stäben keine Welt.

Der weiche Gang geschmeidig starker Schritte,
der sich im allerkleinsten Kreise dreht,
ist wie ein Tanz von Kraft um eine Mitte,
in der betäubt ein großer Wille steht.

Nur manchmal schiebt der Vorhang der Pupille
sich lautlos auf—. Dann geht ein Bild hinein,
geht durch der Glieder angespannte Stille—
und hört im Herzen auf zu sein.

The Panther

In the Jardin des Plantes, Paris

His gaze has from the passing of the bars
become so tired, that it holds nothing more.
It seems to him there are a thousand bars
and behind a thousand bars no world.

The supple pace of powerful soft strides,
turning in the very smallest circle,
is like a dance of strength around a center
in which a great will stands numbed.

Only sometimes the curtain of the pupils
soundlessly slides up—. Then an image enters,
goes through the limbs' taut stillness—
and in the heart ceases to exist.

↓

*... passes through the titan silence
of the shoulders
Reaches the heart, and dies.*

Die Gazelle

Gazella Dorcas

Verzauberte: wie kann der Einklang zweier
erwählter Worte je den Reim erreichen,
der in dir kommt und geht, wie auf ein Zeichen.
Aus deiner Stirne steigen Laub und Leier,

und alles Deine geht schon im Vergleich
durch Liebeslieder, deren Worte, weich
wie Rosenblätter, dem, der nicht mehr liest,
sich auf die Augen legen, die er schließt:

um dich zu sehen: hingetragen, als
wäre mit Sprüngen jeder Lauf geladen
und schösse nur nicht ab, solang der Hals

das Haupt ins Horchen hält: wie wenn beim Baden
im Wald die Badende sich unterbricht:
den Waldsee im gewendeten Gesicht.

The Gazelle

Gazella Dorcas

Enchanted one: how shall the concord
of two chosen words attain that rhyme
which ripples through you like a spell?
From your forehead rise leaf and lyre,

and all you are already moves in simile
through songs of love, whose words, softly
like rose petals, settle on the gaze of one
who, no longer reading, closes his eyes:

to see you there: brought all at once, as
if each limb were charged with leaps and only
kept from firing for the time your neck

holds your head listening: as when, bathing
in a forest, a girl hears something stir:
the lake's reflection in her quick-turned face.

Das Einhorn

Der Heilige hob das Haupt, und das Gebet
fiel wie ein Helm zurück von seinem Haupte:
denn lautlos nahte sich das niegeglaubte,
das weiße Tier, das wie eine geraubte
hülflose Hindin mit den Augen fleht.

Der Beine elfenbeinernes Gestell
bewegte sich in leichten Gleichgewichten,
ein weißer Glanz glitt selig durch das Fell,
und auf der Tierstirn, auf der stillen, lichten,
stand, wie ein Turm im Mond, das Horn so hell,
und jeder Schritt geschah, es aufzurichten.

Das Maul mit seinem rosagrauen Flaum
war leicht gerafft, so daß ein wenig Weiß
(weißer als alles) von den Zähnen glänzte;
die Nüstern nahmen auf und lechzten leis.
Doch seine Blicke, die kein Ding begrenzte,
warfen sich Bilder in den Raum
und schlossen einen blauen Sagenkreis.

The Unicorn

The saint looked up, and the prayer
fell back like a helmet from his head:
for soundlessly the never-believed-in neared,
the white animal, that like an abducted
helpless hind pleads with its eyes.

The thin legs' ivory undercarriage
moved in easy equilibrium,
a white gleam slid blissfully through the coat,
and on the clear, smooth animal brow
the bright horn stood, like a moonlit tower,
and each step carried it erect.

The muzzle with its rose-gray down
was slightly drawn, so that a bit of white
(whitest of all) gleamed from the teeth;
the nostrils drew in and gently languished.
But its gaze, which no thing impeded,
cast images into space
and closed out a blue legend-cycle.

Sankt Sebastian

Wie ein Liegender so steht er; ganz
hingehalten von dem großen Willen.
Weitentrückt wie Mütter, wenn sie stillen,
und in sich gebunden wie ein Kranz.

Und die Pfeile kommen: jetzt und jetzt
und als sprängen sie aus seinen Lenden,
eisern bebend mit den freien Enden.
Doch er lächelt dunkel, unverletzt.

Einmal nur wird seine Trauer groß,
und die Augen liegen schmerzlich bloß,
bis sie etwas leugnen, wie Geringes,
und als ließen sie verächtlich los
die Vernichter eines schönen Dinges.

Saint Sebastian

Like someone lying down he stands there;
entirely held out by his great will.
Far removed, like mothers when they suckle,
and bound into himself like a wreath.

And the arrows come: *now* and *now*
and as if they sprang out of his own loins,
stiffly trembling with their free ends.
But he smiles darkly, unharmed.

Only once does his sorrow become great,
and his eyes lie painfully bare,
until they deny something, as if trivial,
and as if they scornfully let go
the destroyers of a beautiful thing.

Der Stifter

Das war der Auftrag an die Malergilde.
Vielleicht daß ihm der Heiland nie erschien;
vielleicht trat auch kein heiliger Bischof milde
an seine Seite wie in diesem Bilde
und legte leise seine Hand auf ihn.

Vielleicht war dieses alles: *so* zu knien
(so wie es alles ist was wir erfuhren):
zu knien: daß man die eigenen Konturen,
die auswärtswollenden, ganz angespannt
im Herzen hält, wie Pferde in der Hand.

Daß wenn ein Ungeheueres geschähe,
das nicht versprochen ist und nieverbrieft,
wir hoffen könnten, daß es uns nicht sähe
und näher käme, ganz in unsre Nähe,
mit sich beschäftigt und in sich vertieft.

The Donor

That was the commission to the painters' guild.
Perhaps the Saviour never appeared to him;
perhaps even no holy bishop stepped
gently to his side as in this painting
and lightly placed his hand on him.

Perhaps this was everything: *thus* to kneel
(just as it's all that we experienced):
to kneel: and thereby hold one's own
outward-willing contours tightly reined
in one's heart, like horses in one's hand.

So that if something enormous should happen,
something unpromised and never-written,
we could hope that it wouldn't see us
and would come closer, all the way up to us,
deep in itself and self-occupied.

Der Engel

Mit einem Neigen seiner Stirne weist
er weit von sich was einschränkt und verpflichtet;
denn durch sein Herz geht riesig aufgerichtet
das ewig Kommende das kreist.

Die tiefen Himmel stehn ihm voll Gestalten,
und jede kann ihm rufen: komm, erkenn—.
Gieb seinen leichten Händen nichts zu halten
aus deinem Lastenden. Sie kämen denn

bei Nacht zu dir, dich ringender zu prüfen,
und gingen wie Erzürnte durch das Haus
und griffen dich als ob sie dich erschüfen
und brächen dich aus deiner Form heraus.

The Angel

With a slight tilt of his forehead he rejects
everything that hems in and obliges;
for the wide circles of the eternal Coming
move hugely erected through his heart.

The deep heavens stand before him full of shapes,
and each may call to him: come, know me—.
Give his light hands nothing to hold
of your burdens. Otherwise they'll come at night

to you, to test you with a fiercer grip,
and go like someone angry through your house
and seize you as if they'd created you
and break you out of your mold.

Römische Sarkophage

Was aber hindert uns zu glauben, daß
(so wie wir hingestellt sind und verteilt)
nicht eine kleine Zeit nur Drang und Haß
und dies Verwirrende in uns verweilt,

wie einst in dem verzierten Sarkophag
bei Ringen, Götterbildern, Gläsern, Bändern,
in langsam sich verzehrenden Gewändern
ein langsam Aufgelöstes lag—

bis es die unbekannten Munde schluckten,
die niemals reden. (Wo besteht und denkt
ein Hirn, um ihrer einst sich zu bedienen?)

Da wurde von den alten Aquädukten
ewiges Wasser in sie eingelenkt—:
das spiegelt jetzt und geht und glänzt in ihnen.

Roman Sarcophagi

But what prevents us from believing, that
(the way we're scattered out and set in place)
only for a short time thirst and hatred
and this confusion dwell inside us,

as once in this ornate sarcophagus,
among rings, glasses, ribbons, images of gods,
inside slowly self-consuming garments
a slowly loosened something lay—

till it was swallowed by those unknown mouths
that never speak. (Where exists and thinks
a brain that one day will make use of them?)

Then from the ancient aqueducts
eternal water was steered into them—:
which mirrors in them now and moves and shines.

Der Schwan

Diese Mühsal, durch noch Ungetanes
schwer und wie gebunden hinzugehn,
gleicht dem ungeschaffnen Gang des Schwanes.

Und das Sterben, dieses Nichtmehrfassen
jenes Grunds, auf dem wir täglich stehn,
seinem ängstlichen Sich-Niederlassen—:

in die Wasser, die ihn sanft empfangen
und die sich, wie glücklich und vergangen,
unter ihm zurückziehn, Flut um Flut;
während er unendlich still und sicher
immer mündiger und königlicher
und gelassener zu ziehn geruht.

The Swan

This toil and struggle—passing on, heavy
and as if bound, through things still undone,
is like the makeshift walking of the swan.

And dying—this no longer grasping
of that ground, on which we daily stand,
like his nervous settling himself—:

into the water, which received him gently,
and which, so happy in its passing,
draws back under him, wave after wave;
while he, infinitely still and sure,
ever more confidently and majestically
and serenely deigns to glide.

Kindheit

Es wäre gut viel nachzudenken, um
von so Verlornem etwas auszusagen,
von jenen langen Kindheit-Nachmittagen,
die so nie wiederkamen—und warum?

Noch mahnt es uns—: vielleicht in einem Regnen,
aber wir wissen nicht mehr was das soll;
nie wieder war das Leben von Begegnen,
von Wiedersehn und Weitergehn so voll

wie damals, da uns nichts geschah als nur
was einem Ding geschieht und einem Tiere:
da lebten wir, wie Menschliches, das Ihre
und wurden bis zum Rande voll Figur.

Und wurden so vereinsamt wie ein Hirt
und so mit großen Fernen überladen
und wie von weit berufen und berührt
und langsam wie ein langer neuer Faden
in jene Bilder-Folgen eingeführt,
in welchen nun zu dauern uns verwirrt.

Childhood

It would be good to give much thought, before
you try to find words for what is so lost,
for those long childhood afternoons you knew
that never came back again—and why?

There are still reminders—: perhaps in a rain,
but we no longer know what they mean;
never again was life so filled with meeting,
with reuniting and with moving off

as then, when nothing happened to us except
what happens to things and to animals:
we lived then, as humanness, what was theirs,
and became brimful with primal figures.

And became as lonely as a shepherd
and as overburdened by vast distances
and as if from far off summoned and stirred
and slowly like a long new thread
introduced into that picture sequence
in which now going on bewilders us.

Der Dichter

Du entfernst dich von mir, du Stunde.
Wunden schlägt mir dein Flügelschlag.
Allein: was soll ich mit meinem Munde?
mit meiner Nacht? mit meinem Tag?

Ich habe keine Geliebte, kein Haus,
keine Stelle auf der ich lebe.
Alle Dinge, an die ich mich gebe,
werden reich und geben mich aus.

The Poet

You're withdrawing from me, you hour.
The beating of your wings leaves me bruised.
Alone: what shall I do with my mouth?
with my night? with my day?

I have no loved one, no house,
no place to lead a life.
All the things to which I give myself
grow rich and spend me.

Die Spitze

I

Menschlichkeit: Namen schwankender Besitze,
noch unbestätigter Bestand von Glück:
ist das unmenschlich, daß zu dieser Spitze,
zu diesem kleinen dichten Spitzenstück
zwei Augen wurden?—Willst du sie zurück?

Du Langvergangene und schließlich Blinde,
ist deine Seligkeit in diesem Ding,
zu welcher hin, wie zwischen Stamm und Rinde,
dein großes Fühlen, kleinverwandelt, ging?

Durch einen Riß im Schicksal, eine Lücke
entzogst du deine Seele deiner Zeit;
und sie ist so in diesem lichten Stücke,
daß es mich lächeln macht vor Nützlichkeit.

The Lace

Humanness: name for wavering possession,
still unconfirmed continuance of luck:
is it inhuman that for this lace's making,
this small dense needless piece of lace,
two eyes were paid?—Do you want them back?

You long departed and finally blind,
does your bliss live on within this thing,
into which, as between trunk and bark,
your great feeling, grown minuscule, went?

Through a rip in fate, a tiny hole,
you extracted from your time your soul;
and it inheres so in this lucid work,
that when I think of "usefulness" I smile.

II

Und wenn uns eines Tages dieses Tun
und was an uns geschieht gering erschiene
und uns so fremd, als ob es nicht verdiene,
daß wir so mühsam aus den Kinderschuhn
um seinetwillen wachsen—: Ob die Bahn
vergilbter Spitze, diese dichtgefügte
blumige Spitzenbahn, dann nicht genügte,
uns hier zu halten? Sieh: sie ward *getan*.

Ein Leben ward vielleicht verschmäht, wer weiß?
Ein Glück war da und wurde hingegeben,
und endlich wurde doch, um jeden Preis,
dies Ding daraus, nicht leichter als das Leben
und doch vollendet und so schön als sei's
nicht mehr zu früh, zu lächeln und zu schweben.

II

And if one day this doing and all
that involves us here should seem petty
and estranged, as if not recompense
for how we toil so for its sake to grow
out of childhood's shoes—: Would this piece
of yellowed lace, this tightly woven
length of flowery lace, not then suffice
to hold us here? Look: it was *done*.

A life perhaps was spurned, who knows?
A chance at happiness was there and given up,
and yet finally, at whatever price,
this *thing* grew out of it, not easier than life
and yet completed and so perfect—as if
it were no longer too soon to laugh and soar.

Ein Frauen-Schicksal

So wie der König auf der Jagd ein Glas
ergreift, daraus zu trinken, irgendeines,—
und wie hernach der welcher es besaß
es fortstellt und verwahrt als wär es keines:

so hob vielleicht das Schicksal, durstig auch,
bisweilen Eine an den Mund und trank,
die dann ein kleines Leben, viel zu bang
sie zu zerbrechen, abseits vom Gebrauch

hinstellte in die ängstliche Vitrine,
in welcher seine Kostbarkeiten sind
(oder die Dinge, die für kostbar gelten).

Da stand sie fremd wie eine Fortgeliehne
und wurde einfach alt und wurde blind
und war nicht kostbar und war niemals selten.

A Woman's Fate

Just as the king out on a hunt picks up
a glass to drink from, any one at all,—
and afterwards he who owns it puts it away
and guards it like some fabled chalice:

so perhaps Fate, thirsty also, at times
raised a woman to its lips and drank,
whom then a small life, far too afraid
of breaking her, put away from use

inside the fastidious glass cupboard
in which its most precious things are kept
(or the things that count as precious).

There she stood strange like something loaned
and became merely old and became blind
and was not precious and was never special.

Die Genesende

Wie ein Singen kommt und geht in Gassen
und sich nähert und sich wieder scheut,
flügelschlagend, manchmal fast zu fassen
und dann wieder weit hinausgestreut:

spielt mit der Genesenden das Leben;
während sie, geschwächt und ausgeruht,
unbeholfen, um sich hinzugeben,
eine ungewohnte Geste tut.

Und sie fühlt es beinah wie Verführung,
wenn die hartgewordne Hand, darin
Fieber waren voller Widersinn,
fernher, wie mit blühender Berührung,
zu liebkosen kommt ihr hartes Kinn.

The Convalescent

As a singing comes and goes in the streets
and draws near and once again shies off,
fluttering, sometimes almost to be grasped
and then once again scattered out wide:

life is playing with the convalescent;
while she, weakened and rested,
clumsily, in order to devote herself,
makes an unaccustomed gesture.

And she feels it almost like seduction
when her hardened hand, in which
fevers once burned full of nonsense,
from far off, as if with blossoming touch,
comes to caress her hard-set chin.

Die Erwachsene

Das alles stand auf ihr und war die Welt
und stand auf ihr mit allem, Angst und Gnade,
wie Bäume stehen, wachsend und gerade,
ganz Bild und bildlos wie die Bundeslade
und feierlich, wie auf ein Volk gestellt.

Und sie ertrug es; trug bis obenhin
das Fliegende, Entfliehende, Entfernte,
das Ungeheuere, noch Unerlernte
gelassen wie die Wasserträgerin
den vollen Krug. Bis mitten unterm Spiel,
verwandelnd und auf andres vorbereitend,
der erste weiße Schleier, leise gleitend,
über das aufgetane Antlitz fiel

fast undurchsichtig und sich nie mehr hebend
und irgendwie auf alle Fragen ihr
nur eine Antwort vage wiedergebend:
In dir, du Kindgewesene, in dir.

The Grownup

That all stood on her and was the world
and stood on her with all its dread and grace
the way trees stand, growing and erect,
all image and imageless like the Ark of God
and solemnly, as if placed upon a nation.

And she bore it; bore high overhead
the flying, the fleeting, the far-receding,
the prodigious, the still-unlearned
serenely as the water-carrier
her brimful jug. Till in the midst of play,
changing and making ready for other things,
the first white veil, lightly gliding,
fell over her opened face

almost opaque and never again lifting
and somehow to all questions
returning to her vaguely just one answer:
in you, you one-time-child, in you.

Tanagra

Ein wenig gebrannter Erde,
wie von großer Sonne gebrannt.
Als wäre die Gebärde
einer Mädchenhand
auf einmal nicht mehr vergangen;
ohne nach etwas zu langen,
zu keinem Dinge hin
aus ihrem Gefühle führend,
nur an sich selber rührend
wie eine Hand ans Kinn.

Wir heben und wir drehen
eine und eine Figur;
wir können fast verstehen
weshalb sie nicht vergehen,—
aber wir sollen nur
tiefer und wunderbarer
hängen an dem was war
und lächeln: ein wenig klarer
vielleicht als vor einem Jahr.

Tanagra

A bit of baked earth,
baked as by a mighty sun.
As if the gesture
that a girl's hand makes
had suddenly remained:
without reaching for anything,
leading from its feeling
toward no object,
only touching itself
like a hand raised to a chin.

We lift and we keep turning
the same few figures;
we can almost understand
why they don't perish,—
but we're meant only
more deeply and wonderingly
to cling to what once was
and smile: a bit more clearly
perhaps than a year before.

Tanagra: a city of ancient Greece, and the origin of a group of small clay fig-
ures preserved in the Louvre. Writing of them to his wife (26 September
1902), Rilke remarked: "And then Tanagra. It is the source of imperishable
life."

Die Erblindende

Sie saß so wie die anderen beim Tee.
Mir war zuerst, als ob sie ihre Tasse
ein wenig anders als die andern fasse.
Sie lächelte einmal. Es tat fast weh.

Und als man schließlich sich erhob und sprach
und langsam und wie es der Zufall brachte
durch viele Zimmer ging (man sprach und lachte),
da sah ich sie. Sie ging den andern nach,

verhalten, so wie eine, welche gleich
wird singen müssen und vor vielen Leuten;
auf ihren hellen Augen die sich freuten
war Licht von außen wie auf einem Teich.

Sie folgte langsam und sie brauchte lang
als wäre etwas noch nicht überstiegen;
und doch: als ob, nach einem Übergang,
sie nicht mehr gehen würde, sondern fliegen.

Going Blind

She sat just like the others having tea.
I sensed first how she seemed to hold her cup
a little differently from the others.
She smiled once. It almost hurt.

And when they finally rose and spoke
and slowly and as chance would have it
walked through many rooms (they talked and laughed),
I saw her there. She walked behind the others,

restrained, like one who in a moment
will have to sing and before many people;
on her bright eyes that were rejoicing
there was light from outside as on a pond.

She followed slowly and she needed time
as if there were something still not surmounted;
and yet: as if, after a crossing over,
she would no longer walk, but fly.

In einem fremden Park

Borgeby-Gård

Zwei Wege sinds. Sie führen keinen hin.
Doch manchmal, in Gedanken, läßt der eine
dich weitergehn. Es ist, als gingst du fehl;
aber auf einmal bist du im Rondel
alleingelassen wieder mit dem Steine
und wieder auf ihm lesend: Freiherrin
Brite Sophie—und wieder mit dem Finger
abfühlend die zerfallne Jahreszahl—.
Warum wird dieses Finden nicht geringer?

Was zögerst du ganz wie zum ersten Mal
erwartungsvoll auf diesem Ulmenplatz,
der feucht und dunkel ist und niebetreten?

Und was verlockt dich für ein Gegensatz,
etwas zu suchen in den sonnigen Beeten,
als wärs der Name eines Rosenstocks?

Was stehst du oft? Was hören deine Ohren?
Und warum siehst du schließlich, wie verloren,
die Falter flimmern um den hohen Phlox.

In a Foreign Park

Borgeby-Gård

There are two paths. Neither takes you.
Sometimes, though, lost in thought, the one
lets you go on. It's as if you'd erred;
yet suddenly you're in the ring of flowers
left alone again with the stone
and again reading on it: Baroness
Brita-Sophie—and again with your finger
feeling out the ruined date—.
Why does this discovery not grow stale?

Why do you pause just like the first time
so expectantly in this plot of elms,
which is damp and dark and never entered?

And what counter-urging lures you
to search for something in the sunny beds,
as though the name of a rose tree?

Why do you keep stopping? What do you hear?
And why do you finally see, as if lost,
moths flickering around the tall phlox?

Abschied

Wie hab ich das gefühlt was Abschied heißt.
Wie weiß ichs noch: ein dunkles unverwundnes
grausames Etwas, das ein Schönverbundnes
noch einmal zeigt und hinhält und zerreißt.

Wie war ich ohne Wehr, dem zuzuschauen,
das, da es mich, mich rufend, gehen ließ,
zurückblieb, so als wärens alle Frauen
und dennoch klein und weiß und nichts als dies:

Ein Winken, schon nicht mehr auf mich bezogen,
ein leise Weiterwinkendes—, schon kaum
erklärbar mehr: vielleicht ein Pflaumenbaum,
von dem ein Kuckuck hastig abgeflogen.

Farewell

How I have felt the shape that "farewell" takes.
How I know it yet: a dark unvanquished
cruel something, by which a tender coalescence
is once more shown and held and torn apart.

How exposed I was, gazing on at that
which, as it, calling me, released its hold,
stayed behind, as if it were every woman
yet small and white and nothing more than this:

a waving, already no longer linked to me,
a something faintly waving on—, already scarcely
explainable any more: perhaps a plum branch
from which a cuckoo has hastily flown away.

Todes-Erfahrung

Wir wissen nichts von diesem Hingehn, das
nicht mit uns teilt. Wir haben keinen Grund,
Bewunderung und Liebe oder Haß
dem Tod zu zeigen, den ein Maskenmund

tragischer Klage wunderlich entstellt.
Noch ist die Welt voll Rollen, die wir spielen.
Solang wir sorgen, ob wir auch gefielen,
spielt auch der Tod, obwohl er nicht gefällt.

Doch als du gingst, da brach in diese Bühne
ein Streifen Wirklichkeit durch jenen Spalt
durch den du hingingst: Grün wirklicher Grüne,
wirklicher Sonnenschein, wirklicher Wald.

Wir spielen weiter. Bang und schwer Erlerntes
hersagend und Gebärden dann und wann
aufhebend; aber dein von uns entferntes,
aus unserm Stück entrücktes Dasein kann

uns manchmal überkommen, wie ein Wissen
von jener Wirklichkeit sich niedersenkend,
so daß wir eine Weile hingerissen
das Leben spielen, nicht an Beifall denkend.

Death Experienced

We know nothing of this going-hence that
does not share with us. We have no grounds
for showing admiration and love or hate
to death, whom a costume mask

of tragic lament crazily disfigures.
Still the world is full of roles we act.
So long as we try anxiously to please,
death acts also, though never to acclaim.

But when you went, a streak of reality
broke in upon this stage through that fissure
where you left: green of real green,
real sunshine, real forest.

We go on acting. Fearful and reciting
things difficult to learn and now and then
raising gestures; but your existence,
withdrawn from us and taken from our play,

can sometimes come over us, like a knowledge
of that reality settling in,
so that for a while we act life
transported, not thinking of applause.

Blaue Hortensie

So wie das letzte Grün in Farbentiegeln
sind diese Blätter, trocken, stumpf und rauh,
hinter den Blütendolden, die ein Blau
nicht auf sich tragen, nur von ferne spiegeln.

Sie spiegeln es verweint und ungenau,
als wollten sie es wiederum verlieren,
und wie in alten blauen Briefpapieren
ist Gelb in ihnen, Violett und Grau;

Verwaschnes wie an einer Kinderschürze,
Nichtmehrgetragnes, dem nichts mehr geschieht:
wie fühlt man eines kleinen Lebens Kürze.

Doch plötzlich scheint das Blau sich zu verneuen
in einer von den Dolden, und man sieht
ein rührend Blaues sich vor Grünem freuen.

Blue Hydrangea

These leaves are like the last green
in the paint pans, dried-out, dull, and rough,
behind the umbelled blossoms that are a blue
they do not bear, only mirror from far away.

They mirror it tear-stained and inexactly,
as if they wished in turn to lose it;
and as in sheets of old blue letter paper
there's yellow in them, violet and gray;

washed out as with a childhood apron,
the no-longer-worn that nothing more befalls:
how one feels a small life's shortness.

But suddenly the blue seems to revive
in one of the umbels, and you see
a touching blue's delight in greenness.

Vor dem Sommerregen

Auf einmal ist aus allem Grün im Park
man weiß nicht was, ein Etwas, fortgenommen;
man fühlt ihn näher an die Fenster kommen
und schweigsam sein. Inständig nur und stark

ertönt aus dem Gehölz der Regenpfeifer,
man denkt an einen Hieronymus:
so sehr steigt irgend Einsamkeit und Eifer
aus dieser einen Stimme, die der Guß

erhören wird. Des Saales Wände sind
mit ihren Bildern von uns fortgetreten,
als dürften sie nicht hören was wir sagen.

Es spiegeln die verblichenen Tapeten
das ungewisse Licht von Nachmittagen,
in denen man sich fürchtete als Kind.

Before the Summer Rain

Suddenly from all the green in the park
something—you can't say what—has been withdrawn;
you feel the park come closer to the window
and grow taciturn. From the copse

the plover's call rings out, urgent and strong,
reminding you of a Saint Jerome:
so intense a solitude and zeal rises
from that one voice, to which the downpour

will respond. The walls of the great hall have
with their pictures moved away from us,
as if they weren't to hear what we might say.

The faded tapestries reflect
that uncertain light of afternoons,
in which you grew frightened as a child.

Im Saal

Wie sind sie alle um uns, diese Herrn
in Kammerherrentrachten und Jabots,
wie eine Nacht um ihren Ordensstern
sich immer mehr verdunkelnd, rücksichtslos,
und diese Damen, zart, fragile, doch groß
von ihren Kleidern, eine Hand im Schooß,
klein wie ein Halsband für den Bologneser:
wie sind sie da um jeden: um den Leser,
um den Betrachter dieser Bibelots,
darunter manches ihnen noch gehört.

Sie lassen, voller Takt, uns ungestört
das Leben leben wie wir es begreifen
und wie sie's nicht verstehn. Sie wollten blühn,
und blühn ist schön sein; doch wir wollen reifen,
und das heißt dunkel sein und sich bemühn.

In the Hall

How they are all around us, these lords
in chamberlain's attire and frilled shirts,
like a night around its order-star
becoming ever darker, remorselessly,
and these ladies, slight, fragile, yet large
in their dresses, one hand in their laps,
small as the collar for a tiny hound:
how they are here around each one: around the reader,
around the peruser of these trinkets,
many of which still belong to them.

Full of tact, they allow us undisturbed
to live life as we conceive it and as they
don't understand it. They wanted to blossom,
and blossoming is being beautiful; but we want to ripen,
and that means being dark and taking pains.

Letzter Abend

(Aus dem Besitze Frau Nonnas)

Und Nacht und fernes Fahren; denn der Train
des ganzen Heeres zog am Park vorüber.
Er aber hob den Blick vom Clavecin
und spielte noch und sah zu ihr hinüber

beinah wie man in einen Spiegel schaut:
so sehr erfüllt von seinen jungen Zügen
und wissend, wie sie seine Trauer trügen,
schön und verführender bei jedem Laut.

Doch plötzlich wars, als ob sich das verwische:
sie stand wie mühsam in der Fensternische
und hielt des Herzens drängendes Geklopf.

Sein Spiel gab nach. Von draußen wehte Frische.
Und seltsam fremd stand auf dem Spiegeltische
der schwarze Tschako mit dem Totenkopf.

Last Evening

(By permission of Frau Nonna)

And night and distant travel: for the train
of the entire army drew past the park.
But he raised his eyes from the clavichord
and played on and gazed across to her

almost as one looks into a mirror:
so intensely filled with his young features
and knowing how they bore his sadness,
beautifully and more seductively with each sound.

But suddenly it was as if that blurred:
she stood as if with effort in the window niche
and held back her heart's urgent beating.

His play gave way. From outside a crisp wind blew.
And strangely foreign on the mirror table
stood the jet-black shako with the death's-head.

Jugend-Bildnis meines Vaters

Im Auge Traum. Die Stirn wie in Berührung
mit etwas Fernem. Um den Mund enorm
viel Jugend, ungelächelte Verführung,
und vor der vollen schmückenden Verschnürung
der schlanken adeligen Uniform
der Säbelkorb und beide Hände—, die
abwarten, ruhig, zu nichts hingedrängt.
Und nun fast nicht mehr sichtbar: als ob sie
zuerst, die Fernes greifenden, verschwänden.
Und alles andre mit sich selbst verhängt
und ausgelöscht als ob wirs nicht verständen
und tief aus seiner eignen Tiefe trüb—.

Du schnell vergehendes Daguerreotyp
in meinen langsamer vergehenden Händen.

Portrait of My Father as a Young Man

In the eyes dream. The brow as if in touch
with something far away. About the lips
immense youth, unsmiling seductiveness,
and across the full ornamental braids
of the slim aristocratic uniform
the saber's hilt and both the hands—,
waiting, calmly, urged toward nothing.
And now scarcely visible: as if they would be
first, grasping the Distant, to disappear.
And all the rest self-shrouded
and erased as if we didn't understand
and deeply out of its own depths clouded.

You swiftly fading daguerreotype
in my more slowly fading hands.

Selbstbildnis aus dem Jahre 1906

Des alten lange adligen Geschlechtes
Feststehendes im Augenbogenbau.
Im Blicke noch der Kindheit Angst und Blau
und Demut da und dort, nicht eines Knechtes
doch eines Dienenden und einer Frau.
Der Mund als Mund gemacht, groß und genau,
nicht überredend, aber ein Gerechtes
Aussagendes. Die Stirne ohne Schlechtes
und gern im Schatten stiller Niederschau.

Das, als Zusammenhang, erst nur geahnt;
noch nie im Leiden oder im Gelingen
zusammgefaßt zu dauerndem Durchdringen,
doch so, als wäre mit zerstreuten Dingen
von fern ein Ernstes, Wirkliches geplant.

Self-Portrait from the Year 1906

The old long-noble family's
staying power in the eyebrows' build.
In the gaze still the childhood fear and blue
and humility here and there, not slavish
but a server's and a woman's.
The mouth made as mouth, large and exact,
not for persuading but for some just cause's
speaking-out. The forehead without guile
and happy in the shadows of quiet down-gazing.

This, as coherence, just barely sensed;
never as yet in sorrow or success
drawn together for lasting penetration,
but rather as if from far off with scattered things
something serious, real were being planned.

Der König

Der König ist sechzehn Jahre alt.
Sechzehn Jahre und schon der Staat.
Er schaut, wie aus einem Hinterhalt,
vorbei an den Greisen vom Rat

in den Saal hinein und irgendwohin
und fühlt vielleicht nur dies:
an dem schmalen langen harten Kinn
die kalte Kette vom Vlies.

Das Todesurteil vor ihm bleibt
lang ohne Namenszug.
Und sie denken: wie er sich quält.

Sie wüßten, kennten sie ihn genug,
daß er nur langsam bis siebzig zählt
eh er es unterschreibt.

The King

The king is sixteen years old.
Sixteen years and already the state.
He gazes, as from an ambush,
past the graybeards of the council

somewhere into the hall beyond
and feels perhaps only this:
on his narrow, long, hard chin
the cold chain of the Fleece.

The death sentence in front of him remains
for a long time unsigned.
And they think: how he agonizes.

They'd know, if they knew him well enough,
that he just slowly counts to seventy
before he initials it.

Auferstehung

Der Graf vernimmt die Töne,
er sieht einen lichten Riß;
er weckt seine dreizehn Söhne
im Erb-Begräbnis.

Er grüßt seine beiden Frauen
ehrerbietig von weit—;
und alle, voll Vertrauen,
stehn auf zur Ewigkeit

und warten nur noch auf Erich
und Ulriken Dorotheen,
die, sieben- und dreizehnjährig,
   (sechzehnhundertzehn)
verstorben sind im Flandern,
um heute vor den andern
unbeirrt herzugehn.

Resurrection

The Count hears sounds erupting,
he sees a gleaming rift,
he wakes his thirteen sons
in the family crypt.

He welcomes both of his wives
respectfully from afar—;
and all, full of confidence,
arise for Eternity

and wait only for Eric
and Ulrica Dorothea,
who, seventeen and thirteen,
    (sixteen hundred ten)
died far away in Flanders,
so that today at the head of the others
they will walk forth unperturbed.

Rilke provides a tentative gloss on the last stanza of the poem in a letter to
Hedwig von Boddien (10 August 1913): "Eric and Ulrica Dorothea are
brother and sister of the thirteen sons; because they were the youngest to die,
the place of precedence is reserved for them. That the others are kept waiting
for them is to be explained by the fact that they are buried not in the family
tomb, but in a church in Flanders, where during times of unrest death ac-
costed them. The father, therefore, cannot wake them; they must rise from the
grave on their own. Certainly it will take time for them to emerge from their
quietly accepted slumber and adjust themselves to this new condition; nor
will they, in their childish equanimity and surprise, be possessed by the same
zeal as the adults for this resplendent new turn in their life here or in the be-
yond."

Der Fahnenträger

Die Andern fühlen alles an sich rauh
und ohne Anteil: Eisen, Zeug und Leder.
Zwar manchmal schmeichelt eine weiche Feder,
doch sehr allein und lieb-los ist ein jeder;
er aber trägt—als trüg er eine Frau—
die Fahne in dem feierlichen Kleide.
Dicht hinter ihm geht ihre schwere Seide,
die manchmal über seine Hände fließt.

Er kann allein, wenn er die Augen schließt,
ein Lächeln sehn: er darf sie nicht verlassen.—

Und wenn es kommt in blitzenden Kürassen
und nach ihr greift und ringt und will sie fassen—:

dann darf er sie abreißen von dem Stocke
als riß er sie aus ihrem Mädchentum,
um sie zu halten unterm Waffenrocke.

Und für die Andern ist das Mut und Ruhm.

The Standard Bearer

The others feel everything on them rough
and without pity—iron, cloth, leather.
True, sometimes a white plume flatters them,
but each one is all alone and love-less;
yet he bears—as if he bore a woman—
the standard in its festive dress.
Just behind him he hears its heavy silk,
which sometimes flows over his hands.

He can only, when he closes his eyes,
see a smile: he must never forsake it.

And when they come in flashing breastplates
and grasp for it and strive and try to seize it—:

Then he must tear it from the lance
as if he tore it from its maidenhood,
to hold it beneath his battlecoat.

And for the others that is bravery and fame.

Der letzte Graf von Brederode
entzieht sich türkischer Gefangenschaft

Sie folgten furchtbar; ihren bunten Tod
von ferne nach ihm werfend, während er
verloren floh, nichts weiter als: bedroht.
Die Ferne seiner Väter schien nicht mehr

für ihn zu gelten; denn um so zu fliehn,
genügt ein Tier vor Jägern. Bis der Fluß
aufrauschte nah und blitzend. Ein Entschluß
hob ihn samt seiner Not und machte ihn

wieder zum Knaben fürstlichen Geblütes.
Ein Lächeln adeliger Frauen goß
noch einmal Süßigkeit in sein verfrühtes

vollendetes Gesicht. Er zwang sein Roß,
groß wie sein Herz zu gehn, sein blutdurchglühtes:
es trug ihn in den Strom wie in sein Schloß.

The Last Count of Brederode
Evades Turkish Captivity

They followed fiercely; their motley death
flinging after him from far away, while he
fled lost, nothing else except: threatened.
His fathers' ancient line no longer seemed

to stretch behind him: to flee like this
one becomes a beast before hunters. Until the river
rushed up, loud and flashing. A resolve
raised him along with his distress

and made him again the young boy
of princely blood. A smile of noble women
once more poured sweetness into his too-soon

completed face. He spurred his horse to race
proudly like his own blood-glowing heart:
it bore him into the flood as if into his castle.

Die Kurtisane

Venedigs Sonne wird in meinem Haar
ein Gold bereiten: aller Alchemie
erlauchten Ausgang. Meine Brauen, die
den Brücken gleichen, siehst du sie

hinführen ob der lautlosen Gefahr
der Augen, die ein heimlicher Verkehr
an die Kanäle schließt, so daß das Meer
in ihnen steigt und fällt und wechselt. Wer

mich einmal sah, beneidet meinen Hund,
weil sich auf ihm oft in zerstreuter Pause
die Hand, die nie an keiner Glut verkohlt,

die unverwundbare, geschmückt, erholt—.
Und Knaben, Hoffnungen aus altem Hause,
gehn wie an Gift an meinem Mund zugrund.

The Courtesan

Venice's sun will in my hair
prepare a gold: all alchemy's
illustrious issue. My brows, which
are like her bridges, look at how

they arch the silent danger
of my eyes, which keep a secret commerce
with her canals, so that the sea
rises and falls and changes in them. Who

has seen me once is jealous of my dog,
since often on him in distracted pauses
my hand, not ever charred by any heat,

invulnerable and bejeweled, rests—.
And boys, the hopes of ancient houses,
perish at my mouth as if by poison.

Die Treppe der Orangerie

Versailles

Wie Könige die schließlich nur noch schreiten
fast ohne Ziel, nur um von Zeit zu Zeit
sich den Verneigenden auf beiden Seiten
zu zeigen in des Mantels Einsamkeit—:

so steigt, allein zwischen den Balustraden,
die sich verneigen schon seit Anbeginn,
die Treppe: langsam und von Gottes Gnaden
und auf den Himmel zu und nirgends hin;

als ob sie allen Folgenden befahl
zurückzubleiben, —so daß sie nicht wagen
von ferne nachzugehen; nicht einmal
die schwere Schleppe durfte einer tragen.

The Stairs of the Orangery

Versailles

Like kings who in the end still stride
almost without purpose,—only to appear
from time to time in their mantle's solitude
for the bowing presences on both sides—:

just so, alone between the balustrades,
which have bowed thus since the beginning,
the stairs climb: slowly and by God's Grace
and up toward heaven and leading nowhere:

as if they had ordered all retinue
to stay behind,—so that they don't dare
follow at a distance; not even one
was deigned by them to bear the heavy train.

Der Marmor-Karren

Paris

Auf Pferde, sieben ziehende, verteilt,
verwandelt Niebewegtes sich in Schritte;
denn was hochmütig in des Marmors Mitte
an Alter, Widerstand und All verweilt,

das zeigt sich unter Menschen. Siehe, nicht
unkenntlich, unter irgend einem Namen,
nein: wie der Held das Drängen in den Dramen
erst sichtbar macht und plötzlich unterbricht:

so kommt es durch den stauenden Verlauf
des Tages, kommt in seinem ganzen Staate,
als ob ein großer Triumphator nahte

langsam zuletzt; und langsam vor ihm her
Gefangene, von seiner Schwere schwer.
Und naht noch immer und hält alles auf.

The Marble-Wagon

Paris

Parcelled out, on horses, seven pulling hard,
the never-moved transforms itself in paces;
for what keeps proudly in the marble's core
of age, resistance, and totality,

displays itself among men. And look,
not unrecognizably, under whatever name:
just as the hero's sudden interruption
first makes clear to us the drama's thrust:

so it's coming through the day's jammed-up
course, coming in full pomp and panoply,
as if a mighty conqueror neared in triumph

slowly at the last; and slowly before him
captives, heavy with his weight. And keeps on
coming near and makes everything stop.

Buddha

Schon von ferne fühlt der fremde scheue
Pilger, wie es golden von ihm träuft;
so als hätten Reiche voller Reue
ihre Heimlichkeiten aufgehäuft.

Aber näher kommend wird er irre
vor der Hoheit dieser Augenbraun:
denn das sind nicht ihre Trinkgeschirre
und die Ohrgehänge ihrer Fraun.

Wüßte einer denn zu sagen, welche
Dinge eingeschmolzen wurden, um
dieses Bild auf diesem Blumenkelche

aufzurichten: stummer, ruhiggelber
als ein goldenes und rundherum
auch den Raum berührend wie sich selber.

Buddha

Already from afar the shy expectant
pilgrim feels how it drips from him goldenly;
as if rich tribes full of penitence
had piled up all their secrets.

But coming nearer he grows confused
before the elevation of these eyebrows:
for that is not their drinking cups
and the earrings of their women.

Is there someone, then, who could say
what things *were* melted down, in order
to erect this image on this flower cup:

more hushed, more peacefully yellow
than a golden one and all around
touching space the way it does itself.

Römische Fontäne

Borghese

Zwei Becken, eins das andre übersteigend
aus einem alten runden Marmorrand,
und aus dem oberen Wasser leis sich neigend
zum Wasser, welches unten wartend stand,

dem leise redenden entgegenschweigend
und heimlich, gleichsam in der hohlen Hand,
ihm Himmel hinter Grün und Dunkel zeigend
wie einen unbekannten Gegenstand;

sich selber ruhig in der schönen Schale
verbreitend ohne Heimweh, Kreis aus Kreis,
nur manchmal träumerisch und tropfenweis

sich niederlassend an den Moosbehängen
zum letzten Spiegel, der sein Becken leis
von unten lächeln macht mit Übergängen.

Roman Fountain

Borghese

Two basins, one rising from the other
in the middle of an old marble pool,
and from the one above, water gently bending
to water, which below stands waiting,

receiving the gentle talking in silence
and secretly, as in a hollowed hand,
showing it sky behind green and darkness
like an unfamiliar object; itself

spreading peacefully in the lovely shell
without homesickness, circle out of circle,
just sometimes dreamily and drop by drop

letting itself down on the mossy hangings
to the last mirror, which makes its basin
from underneath smile gently with transitions.

Das Karussell

Jardin du Luxembourg

Mit einem Dach und seinem Schatten dreht
sich eine kleine Weile der Bestand
von bunten Pferden, alle aus dem Land,
das lange zögert, eh es untergeht.
Zwar manche sind an Wagen angespannt,
doch alle haben Mut in ihren Mienen;
ein böser roter Löwe geht mit ihnen
und dann und wann ein weißer Elefant.

Sogar ein Hirsch ist da, ganz wie im Wald,
nur daß er einen Sattel trägt und drüber
ein kleines blaues Mädchen aufgeschnallt.

Und auf dem Löwen reitet weiß ein Junge
und hält sich mit der kleinen heißen Hand,
dieweil der Löwe Zähne zeigt und Zunge.

Und dann und wann ein weißer Elefant.

Und auf den Pferden kommen sie vorüber,
auch Mädchen, helle, diesem Pferdesprunge
fast schon entwachsen; mitten in dem Schwunge
schauen sie auf, irgendwohin, herüber—

Und dann und wann ein weißer Elefant.

Und das geht hin und eilt sich, daß es endet,
und kreist und dreht sich nur und hat kein Ziel.
Ein Rot, ein Grün, ein Grau vorbeigesendet,
ein kleines kaum begonnenes Profil—.
Und manchesmal ein Lächeln, hergewendet,
ein seliges, das blendet und verschwendet
an dieses atemlose blinde Spiel…

The Carousel

Jardin du Luxembourg

With a roof and its shadow it turns
for a little while, this herd of
many-colored horses, all from the land
that hesitates, a long time, before it's gone.
True, some are hitched to coaches,
yet all have courage in their faces;
an angry red lion goes with them
and now and then a white elephant.

Even a stag is there, just as in the woods,
only he wears a saddle and over that
a small blue girl all buckled up.

And on the lion a boy rides in white
and holds on tight with his small hot hand
while the lion bares teeth and tongue.

And now and then a white elephant.

And on the horses they come riding past,
also girls, bright, almost outgrown already
this springing of horses; in the midst of the lunge
they look up, off into space, over here—

And now and then a white elephant.

And it goes by and hurries to its end,
and only circles and turns and has no goal.
A red, a green, a gray sent past,
a small, scarcely started profile—.
And oftentimes a smile, turned this way,
a blissful one, which dazzles and spends itself
on this blind, breathless play . . .

143

Spanische Tänzerin

Wie in der Hand ein Schwefelzündholz, weiß,
eh es zur Flamme kommt, nach allen Seiten
zuckende Zungen streckt—: beginnt im Kreis
naher Beschauer hastig, hell und heiß
ihr runder Tanz sich zuckend auszubreiten.

Und plötzlich ist er Flamme, ganz und gar.

Mit einem Blick entzündet sie ihr Haar
und dreht auf einmal mit gewagter Kunst
ihr ganzes Kleid in diese Feuersbrunst,
aus welcher sich, wie Schlangen die erschrecken,
die nackten Arme wach und klappernd strecken.

Und dann: als würde ihr das Feuer knapp,
nimmt sie es ganz zusamm und wirft es ab
sehr herrisch, mit hochmütiger Gebärde
und schaut: da liegt es rasend auf der Erde
und flammt noch immer und ergiebt sich nicht—.
Doch sieghaft, sicher und mit einem süßen
grüßenden Lächeln hebt sie ihr Gesicht
und stampft es aus mit kleinen festen Füßen.

Spanish Dancer

As in the hand a sulfur match, first white,
stretches flicking tongues on every side
before it bursts in flame—: so in the circle
of close watchers, hot, bright, and eager
her round dance begins to flicker and fan out.

And all at once it is entirely flame.

With a glance she sets her hair ablaze
and whirls suddenly with daring art
her whole dress into this fiery rapture,
out of which, like startled snakes,
her bare arms stretch, alive and clacking.

And then: as if the fire grew tight to her,
she gathers it all up and casts it off
disdainfully, with imperious demeanor
and looks: it lies there raging on the ground
and keeps on flaming and does not give up—.
But triumphant, self-assured, and with a
sweet greeting smile she lifts her face
and stamps it out with little furious feet.

Der Turm

Tour St.-Nicolas, Furnes

Erd-Inneres. Als wäre dort, wohin
du blindlings steigst, erst Erdenoberfläche,
zu der du steigst im schrägen Bett der Bäche,
die langsam aus dem suchenden Gerinn

der Dunkelheit entsprungen sind, durch die
sich dein Gesicht, wie auferstehend, drängt
und die du plötzlich *siehst*, als fiele sie
aus diesem Abgrund, der dich überhängt

und den du, wie er riesig über dir
sich umstürzt in dem dämmernden Gestühle,
erkennst, erschreckt und fürchtend, im Gefühle:
o wenn er steigt, behangen wie ein Stier—:

Da aber nimmt dich aus der engen Endung
windiges Licht. Fast fliegend siehst du hier
die Himmel wieder, Blendung über Blendung,
und dort die Tiefen, wach und voll Verwendung,

und kleine Tage wie bei Patenier,
gleichzeitige, mit Stunde neben Stunde,
durch die die Brücken springen wie die Hunde,
dem hellen Wege immer auf der Spur,

den unbeholfne Häuser manchmal nur
verbergen, bis er ganz im Hintergrunde
beruhigt geht durch Buschwerk und Natur.

The Tower

Tour St.-Nicolas, Furnes

Earth-inwardness. As if there, to where
you blindly climb, were first earth's surface,
toward which you climb in the slanting bed
of rivulets that have slowly issued

from the groping clot of darkness through which
your face presses, as if resurrecting,
and which you suddenly *see*, as if it fell
out of this abyss which overhangs you

and which you, as it gigantically above you
flips over in the glimmering rafters,
recognize, with a rush of terror, feeling:
O if it climbs, hung like a bull—:

But then gusty light takes you from
that narrow ending. Almost flying you see
here the skies again, dazzle on dazzle,
and there the depths, awake and full of use,

and little days as if by Patenir,
simultaneous, with hour next to hour,
through which the bridges leap like dogs,
always on the trace of the bright path

which clumsy houses sometimes just manage
to conceal, until far in the background
it glides relieved through brushwood and open field.

Der Platz

Furnes

Willkürlich von Gewesnem ausgeweitet:
von Wut und Aufruhr, von dem Kunterbunt
das die Verurteilten zu Tod begleitet,
von Buden, von der Jahrmarktsrufer Mund,
und von dem Herzog der vorüberreitet
und von dem Hochmut von Burgund,

(auf allen Seiten Hintergrund):

ladet der Platz zum Einzug seiner Weite
die fernen Fenster unaufhörlich ein,
während sich das Gefolge und Geleite
der Leere langsam an den Handelsreihn

verteilt und ordnet. In die Giebel steigend,
wollen die kleinen Häuser alles sehn,
die Türme vor einander scheu verschweigend,
die immer maßlos hinter ihnen stehn.

The Square

Furnes

Stretched wide arbitrarily by things past:
by rage and riot, by the motley mix
that accompanies the condemned to death,
by stalls, by the market-crier's mouth,
and by the Duke who rides past
and by the arrogance of Burgundy,

(on all sides background):

the square constantly invites the distant
windows to enter its expanse,
while the entourage and escorts
of emptiness slowly assume a place

in the ranks of commerce. Climbing into the gables,
the small houses try to see everything,
uneasily concealing from one another the towers
that loom ever-massively behind them.

Quai du Rosaire

Brügge

Die Gassen haben einen sachten Gang
(wie manchmal Menschen gehen im Genesen
nachdenkend: was ist früher hier gewesen?)
und die an Plätze kommen, warten lang

auf eine andre, die mit einem Schritt
über das abendklare Wasser tritt,
darin, je mehr sich rings die Dinge mildern,
die eingehängte Welt von Spiegelbildern
so wirklich wird wie diese Dinge nie.

Verging nicht diese Stadt? Nun siehst du, wie
(nach einem unbegreiflichen Gesetz)
sie wach und deutlich wird im Umgestellten,
als wäre dort das Leben nicht so selten;
dort hängen jetzt die Gärten groß und gelten,
dort dreht sich plötzlich hinter schnell erhellten
Fenstern der Tanz in den Estaminets.

Und oben blieb?—Die Stille nur, ich glaube,
und kostet langsam und von nichts gedrängt
Beere um Beere aus der süßen Traube
des Glockenspiels, das in den Himmeln hängt.

Quai du Rosaire

Bruges

The streets move forward with a gentle gait
(the way men often walk in convalescence
thinking to themselves: what used to be here?)
and those that come to squares wait long

for another, which with a single step
strides over the evening-clear water,
in which, as the things around it lose their edge,
the in-hung world of mirrored images
grows real in a way those things never are.

Did this city not expire? Now you see how
(according to an ungraspable law)
it wakes and grows clear in the transposed,
as if there life were not so rare;
there the gardens hang now large and current,
there suddenly behind swiftly lit-up
windows the dance in the cafe spins round.

And left above? Only the silence, I believe,
tasting slowly and rushed by nothing
berry after berry from the sweet cluster
of the carillon hanging in the sky.

Bruges· The poem plays throughout on the identity of Bruges as "Bruges la morte," a famous and thriving medieval city which in its wane—owing in part to the loss of its natural harbor—became a symbol of mutability and transience.

Béguinage

Béguinage Sainte-Elisabeth, Brügge

I

Das hohe Tor scheint keine einzuhalten,
die Brücke geht gleich gerne hin und her,
und doch sind sicher alle in dem alten
offenen Ulmenhof und gehn nicht mehr
aus ihren Häusern, als auf jenem Streifen
zur Kirche hin, um besser zu begreifen
warum in ihnen so viel Liebe war.

Dort knieen sie, verdeckt mit reinem Leinen,
so gleich, als wäre nur das Bild der einen
tausendmal im Choral, der tief und klar
zu Spiegeln wird an den verteilten Pfeilern;
und ihre Stimmen gehn den immer steilern
Gesang hinan und werfen sich von dort,
wo es nicht weitergeht, vom letzten Wort,
den Engeln zu, die sie nicht wiedergeben.

Drum sind die unten, wenn sie sich erheben
und wenden, still. Drum reichen sie sich schweigend
mit einem Neigen, Zeigende zu zeigend
Empfangenden, geweihtes Wasser, das
die Stirnen kühl macht und die Munde blaß.

Und gehen dann, verhangen und verhalten,
auf jenem Streifen wieder überquer—
die Jungen ruhig, ungewiß die Alten
und eine Greisin, weilend, hinterher—
zu ihren Häusern, die sie schnell verschweigen
und die sich durch die Ulmen hin von Zeit
zu Zeit ein wenig reine Einsamkeit,
in einer kleinen Scheibe schimmernd, zeigen.

Béguinage

Béguinage Sainte-Elisabeth, Bruges

I

The high gate seems to hold no one back,
the bridge goes both ways just as willingly,
and yet all are secure in the old
open elm court, and no longer go
out of their houses, except on that strip
to church, to better comprehend
why so much love was placed in them.

They kneel there, cloaked with pure linen,
as alike as though the image of just one
were thousandfold in the chorale that deep and clear
grows mirror-like on the supporting pillars;
and their voices go up the ever steeper
hymn and throw themselves from that place
where it does not go on, from the last word,
to the angels, who don't give them back.

Hence those below, when they rise and turn,
are quiet. Hence they reach each other silently
with a nod, gesturers to gesturing
receivers, holy water, which
makes the brow cool and the mouth pale.

And then go, shrouded and restrained,
back again upon that strip—
the young steadily, the old less surely,
and an aged one, lingering, behind—
to their houses, which quickly hide them,
and which through the elms from time to time
show each other a bit of pure solitude
glimmering in a small window pane.

Was aber spiegelt mit den tausend Scheiben
das Kirchenfenster in den Hof hinein,
darin sich Schweigen, Schein und Widerschein
vermischen, trinken, trüben, übertreiben,
phantastisch alternd wie ein alter Wein.

Dort legt sich, keiner weiß von welcher Seite,
Außen auf Inneres und Ewigkeit
auf Immer-Hingehn, Weite über Weite,
erblindend, finster, unbenutzt, verbleit.

Dort bleibt, unter dem schwankenden Dekor
des Sommertags, das Graue alter Winter:
als stünde regungslos ein sanftgesinnter
langmütig lange Wartender dahinter
und eine weinend Wartende davor.

II

What, though, with its thousand panes does
the church window reflect into the court,
in which silence, semblance, and reflection
mingle, drink, grow gloomy, exaggerate,
fantastically aging like an old wine?

Settling there, from which side none can say,
outer rests on inner and eternity
on ever-passing, distance over distance,
obscure, unused, growing blind, sealed tight.

Enduring there, under the summer day's
wavering decor, is ancient winter's gray:
as if there stood waiting motionlessly
a gentle, patient, long-suffering man behind
and a weeping woman in front.

Die Marien-Prozession

Gent

Aus allen Türmen stürzt sich, Fluß um Fluß,
hinwallendes Metall in solchen Massen
als sollte drunten in der Form der Gassen
ein blanker Tag erstehn aus Bronzeguß,

an dessen Rand, gehämmert und erhaben,
zu sehen ist der buntgebundne Zug
der leichten Mädchen und der neuen Knaben,
und wie er Wellen schlug und trieb und trug,
hinabgehalten von dem ungewissen
Gewicht der Fahnen und von Hindernissen
gehemmt, unsichtbar wie die Hand des Herrn;

und drüben plötzlich beinah mitgerissen
vom Aufstieg aufgescheuchter Räucherbecken,
die fliegend, alle sieben, wie im Schrecken
an ihren Silberketten zerrn.

Die Böschung Schauender umschließt die Schiene,
in der das alles stockt und rauscht und rollt:
das Kommende, das Chryselephantine,
aus dem sich zu Balkonen Baldachine
aufbäumen, schwankend im Behang von Gold.

Und sie erkennen über all dem Weißen,
getragen und im spanischen Gewand,

Procession of the Virgin

Ghent

Out of all the towers wave on wave of
surging metal flings itself in such masses
as if down below in the streets' mold
a shining day should arise from bronze ore,

along whose rim, hammered and embossed,
there'd be seen the brightly knotted train
of nimble girls and brand-new boys,
and how its waves drove and pulsed and sustained,
held down by the uncertain weight
of the banners and stemmed by hindrances
invisible like the hand of God;

and over there suddenly almost swept away
by the upsurge of the startled censers,
which, all seven taking flight, as if in terror
pull at their silver chains.

The scarp of onlookers hems the track
in which the whole thing falters and lurches and rolls:
the Oncoming, the Chryselephantine,
out of which baldachins rear up to balconies,
swaying in the fringework of gold.

And they recognize over all the white,
carried high and dressed in Spanish garb,

Chryselephantine Rilke "explained" the word in a letter of 25 July 1907: "Made
out of gold (*chrysos*, Greek) and ivory (*elephas*), and used of the statues of Phi-
dias, which according to the texts were made of these things: here the expres-
sion should help to evoke suddenly, at a stroke, the white-gold aspect of the
procession."

das alte Standbild mit dem kleinen heißen
Gesichte und dem Kinde auf der Hand
und knieen hin, je mehr es naht und naht,
in seiner Krone ahnungslos veraltend
und immer noch das Segnen hölzern haltend
aus dem sich groß gebärdenden Brokat.

Da aber wie es an den Hingeknieten
vorüberkommt, die scheu von unten schaun,
da scheint es seinen Trägern zu gebieten
mit einem Hochziehn seiner Augenbraun,
hochmütig, ungehalten und bestimmt:
so daß sie staunen, stehn und überlegen
und schließlich zögernd gehn. Sie aber nimmt,

in sich die Schritte dieses ganzen Stromes
und geht, allein, wie auf erkannten Wegen
dem Glockendonnern des großoffnen Domes
auf hundert Schultern frauenhaft entgegen.

the old statue with the small hot face
and the child perched on the hand
and kneel down, the more he nears and nears,
in his crown naively growing obsolete,
and still woodenly holding out his blessing
from the grandly gesturing brocade.

But then as he comes moving past
the kneelers, who gaze shyly from below,
he seems to command his bearers
with a quick uplifting of his eyebrows,
haughty, indignant, and decisive:
so that they start, stand, and ponder
and at last hesitantly proceed. She, though, takes

into herself the steps of that whole flood
and goes, alone, as on familiar paths
toward the thundrous pealings of the wide-open cathedral
on a hundred shoulders with womanly aplomb.

Die Insel

Nordsee

I

Die nächste Flut verwischt den Weg im Watt,
und alles wird auf allen Seiten gleich;
die kleine Insel draußen aber hat
die Augen zu; verwirrend kreist der Deich

um ihre Wohner, die in einen Schlaf
geboren werden, drin sie viele Welten
verwechseln, schweigend; denn sie reden selten,
und jeder Satz ist wie ein Epitaph

für etwas Angeschwemmtes, Unbekanntes,
das unerklärt zu ihnen kommt und bleibt.
Und so ist alles was ihr Blick beschreibt

von Kindheit an: nicht auf sie Angewandtes,
zu Großes, Rücksichtsloses, Hergesandtes,
das ihre Einsamkeit noch übertreibt.

The Island

North Sea

I

The next tide wipes across the mud flat's path,
and everything on all sides grows alike;
but the little island out there has closed
its eyes: the dike circles confusingly

around its dwellers, who have been born
into a sleep where they get many worlds
mixed up, silently: for they seldom talk,
and each sentence is like an epitaph

for something washed on shore, unfamiliar,
that comes there unexplained and stays.
And thus it is with all their gaze describes

from childhood on: things not applied to them,
too large, withdrawn, sent from somewhere,
that just exaggerate their solitude.

Als läge er in einem Krater-Kreise
auf einem Mond: ist jeder Hof umdämmt,
und drin die Gärten sind auf gleiche Weise
gekleidet und wie Waisen gleich gekämmt

von jenem Sturm, der sie so rauh erzieht
und tagelang sie bange macht mit Toden.
Dann sitzt man in den Häusern drin und sieht
in schiefen Spiegeln was auf den Kommoden

Seltsames steht. Und einer von den Söhnen
tritt abends vor die Tür und zieht ein Tönen
aus der Harmonika wie Weinen weich;

so hörte ers in einem fremden Hafen—.
Und draußen formt sich eines von den Schafen
ganz groß, fast drohend, auf dem Außendeich.

II
As if it lay inside a crater's circle
on a moon: every farm is dammed around,
and the gardens inside are dressed the same
and all, like orphans, combed the same

by that storm that brings them up so harshly
and for days frightens them with death.
Then one sits in the house and sees
in crooked mirrors what strange objects stand there

on the dressers. And one of the sons
steps toward the door at dusk and draws a sound
from his harmonica softly like weeping;

he heard it that way in a foreign port—.
And outside one of the fleece-clouds grows huge,
almost threatening, on the outer dike.

III

Nah ist nur Innres; alles andre fern.
Und dieses Innere gedrängt und täglich
mit allem überfüllt und ganz unsäglich.
Die Insel ist wie ein zu kleiner Stern

welchen der Raum nicht merkt und stumm zerstört
in seinem unbewußten Furchtbarsein,
so daß er, unerhellt und überhört,
allein

damit dies alles doch ein Ende nehme
dunkel auf einer selbsterfundnen Bahn
versucht zu gehen, blindlings, nicht im Plan
der Wandelsterne, Sonnen und Systeme.

III

Only what's inmost is near; all the rest is far.
And this Inmost is crowded and every day
filled overfull with everything and past all words.
The island is like a tiny star

that Space doesn't notice and silently
lays waste in its unconscious dreadfulness,
so that it, unillumined and ignored,
alone

so that all this might yet come to an end
darkly on its own self-invented course
tries to go on, blindly, not in the scheme
of the planets, suns, and systems.

Hetären-Gräber

In ihren langen Haaren liegen sie
mit braunen, tief in sich gegangenen Gesichtern.
Die Augen zu wie vor zu vieler Ferne.
Skelette, Munde, Blumen. In den Munden
die glatten Zähne wie ein Reise-Schachspiel
aus Elfenbein in Reihen aufgestellt.
Und Blumen, gelbe Perlen, schlanke Knochen,
Hände und Hemden, welkende Gewebe
über dem eingestürzten Herzen. Aber
dort unter jenen Ringen, Talismanen
und augenblauen Steinen (Lieblings-Angedenken)
steht noch die stille Krypta des Geschlechtes,
bis an die Wölbung voll mit Blumenblättern.
Und wieder gelbe Perlen, weitverrollte,—
Schalen gebrannten Tones, deren Bug
ihr eignes Bild geziert hat, grüne Scherben
von Salben-Vasen, die wie Blumen duften,
und Formen kleiner Götter: Hausaltäre,
Hetärenhimmel mit entzückten Göttern.
Gesprengte Gürtel, flache Skarabäen,
kleine Figuren riesigen Geschlechtes,
ein Mund der lacht und Tanzende und Läufer,
goldene Fibeln, kleinen Bogen ähnlich
zur Jagd auf Tier- und Vogelamulette,
und lange Nadeln, zieres Hausgeräte
und eine runde Scherbe roten Grundes,
darauf, wie eines Eingangs schwarze Aufschrift,

Hetaerae-Tombs

In their long hair they lie
with brown faces gone deep into themselves.
The eyes closed, as if before too great a distance.
Skeletons, mouths, flowers. Inside the mouths
the smooth teeth like a pocket chess set
lined up in ivory rows.
And flowers, yellow pearls, slender bones,
hands and tunics, fading fabric
above the caved-in heart. But
there beneath those rings, talismans,
and eye-blue stones (cherished keepsakes),
the silent crypt of the sex still stands,
filled to its vaulted roof with flower petals.
And again yellow pearls, rolled far asunder,—
dishes of baked clay, whose deep curve
their own image has adorned, green shards
of ointment jars that smell like flowers,
and forms of small deities: household altars,
Hetaerae-heavens with enraptured gods!
Unsprung waistbands, flat scarab stones,
small figures' gigantic sexes,
a mouth that laughs and dancing girls and runners,
golden clasps that look like tiny bows
for hunting beast- and bird-shaped amulets,
and long needles, ornamented household things,
and a round potsherd's reddish ground,
on which, like an entranceway's black inscription,

die straffen Beine eines Viergespannes.
Und wieder Blumen, Perlen, die verrollt sind,
die hellen Lenden einer kleinen Leier,
und zwischen Schleiern, die gleich Nebeln fallen,
wie ausgekrochen aus des Schuhes Puppe:
des Fußgelenkes leichter Schmetterling.

So liegen sie mit Dingen angefüllt,
kostbaren Dingen, Steinen, Spielzeug, Hausrat,
zerschlagnem Tand (was alles in sie abfiel),
und dunkeln wie der Grund von einem Fluß.

Flußbetten waren sie,
darüber hin in kurzen schnellen Wellen
(die weiter wollten zu dem nächsten Leben)
die Leiber vieler Jünglinge sich stürzten
und in denen der Männer Ströme rauschten.
Und manchmal brachen Knaben aus den Bergen
der Kindheit, kamen zagen Falles nieder
und spielten mit den Dingen auf dem Grunde,
bis das Gefälle ihr Gefühl ergriff:

Dann füllten sie mit flachem klaren Wasser
die ganze Breite dieses breiten Weges
und trieben Wirbel an den tiefen Stellen;
und spiegelten zum ersten Mal die Ufer
und ferne Vogelrufe—, während hoch
die Sternennächte eines süßen Landes
in Himmel wuchsen, die sich nirgends schlossen.

the stiff legs of a team-of-four.
And again flowers, pearls rolled apart,
the bright loins of a small lyre,
and between veils, which fall like mist,
as if crept forth from the shoe's chrysalis:
the ankle's pale butterfly.

Thus they lie filled up with things—
precious things, jewels, toys, bowls and spoons,
shattered knick-knacks (all that dropped off into them)—
and darken like the bottom of a river.

They *were* riverbeds,
over whom in short, quick waves
(which wanted to go on to the next life)
the bodies of many young men hurled themselves,
and in whom grown men's torrents rushed.
And sometimes boys broke out of the mountains
of childhood, came down in timid falls
and played with the things on the bottom
until the slope gripped their feeling:

Then they filled with shallow clear water
the entire breadth of that wide course
and made eddies swirl at the deep places;
and mirrored for the first time the shore
and distant birdcalls—, while high up
the starry nights of a sweet country
blossomed into heavens that nowhere closed.

Orpheus. Eurydike. Hermes

Das war der Seelen wunderliches Bergwerk.
Wie stille Silbererze gingen sie
als Adern durch sein Dunkel. Zwischen Wurzeln
entsprang das Blut, das fortgeht zu den Menschen,
und schwer wie Porphyr sah es aus im Dunkel.
Sonst war nichts Rotes.

Felsen waren da
und wesenlose Wälder. Brücken über Leeres
und jener große graue blinde Teich,
der über seinem fernen Grunde hing
wie Regenhimmel über einer Landschaft.
Und zwischen Wiesen, sanft und voller Langmut,
erschien des einen Weges blasser Streifen,
wie eine lange Bleiche hingelegt.

Und dieses einen Weges kamen sie.

Voran der schlanke Mann im blauen Mantel,
der stumm und ungeduldig vor sich aussah.
Ohne zu kauen fraß sein Schritt den Weg
in großen Bissen; seine Hände hingen
schwer und verschlossen aus dem Fall der Falten
und wußten nicht mehr von der leichten Leier,
die in die Linke eingewachsen war
wie Rosenranken in den Ast des Ölbaums.
Und seine Sinne waren wie entzweit:

Orpheus. Eurydice. Hermes

That was the souls' strange mine.
Like silent silver ore they wandered
through its dark like veins. Between roots
the blood welled up that makes its way to men,
and it looked hard as porphyry in the dark.
Nothing else was red.

Rocks were there
and unreal forests. Bridges over voids
and that huge gray blind pond
that hung above its distant bed
like rainy sky above a landscape.
And between meadows, soft and full of patience,
the pale stripe of the single path,
laid down like a long pallor being bleached.

And on this single path they came.

In front the slender man in the blue mantle,
who mutely and impatiently looked straight ahead.
Without chewing his stride ate the road
in huge bites; his hands hung
heavy and clenched out of the falling folds
and knew no longer of the light lyre,
which had ingrained itself into his left
like rose tendrils into an olive branch.
And his senses were as if split in two:

indes der Blick ihm wie ein Hund vorauslief,
umkehrte, kam und immer wieder weit
und wartend an der nächsten Wendung stand,—
blieb sein Gehör wie ein Geruch zurück.
Manchmal erschien es ihm als reichte es
bis an das Gehen jener beiden andern,
die folgen sollten diesen ganzen Aufstieg.
Dann wieder wars nur seines Steigens Nachklang
und seines Mantels Wind was hinter ihm war.
Er aber sagte sich, sie kämen doch;
sagte es laut und hörte sich verhallen.
Sie kämen doch, nur wärens zwei
die furchtbar leise gingen. Dürfte er
sich einmal wenden (wäre das Zurückschaun
nicht die Zersetzung dieses ganzen Werkes,
das erst vollbracht wird), müßte er sie sehen,
die beiden Leisen, die ihm schweigend nachgehn:

Den Gott des Ganges und der weiten Botschaft,
die Reisehaube über hellen Augen,
den schlanken Stab hertragend vor dem Leibe
und flügelschlagend an den Fußgelenken;
und seiner linken Hand gegeben: *sie*.

Die So-geliebte, daß aus einer Leier
mehr Klage kam als je aus Klagefrauen;
daß eine Welt aus Klage ward, in der
alles noch einmal da war: Wald und Tal
und Weg und Ortschaft, Feld und Fluß und Tier;
und daß um diese Klage-Welt, ganz so

for while his sight raced ahead like a dog,
turned around, came and again far away
and waiting stood at the next turn, —
his hearing stayed behind like a smell.
Sometimes it seemed to him as if it reached
back to the footsteps of those other two,
who were to follow for this whole ascent.
Then once more it was just his climbing's echo
and his mantle's wind that were behind him.
But he told himself they *did* come,
said it out loud and heard the words die away.
They *did* come, only they were two
who walked with frightening softness. If he
might once turn around (if looking back
were not the crumbling of this entire work,
so near completion), he would *have* to see them,
those two light ones, who followed him in silence:

The god of faring and the distant message,
the travelling hood over shining eyes,
bearing the slender staff before his body,
and beating wings at his ankle joints;
and given to his left hand: *her*.

The one so loved, that out of one lyre
more lament came than ever from lamenting women;
that a world came out of lament, in which
everything once more appeared: wood and vale
and road and village, field and flock and stream;
and that around this lament-world, just as

wie um die andre Erde, eine Sonne
und ein gestirnter stiller Himmel ging,
ein Klage-Himmel mit entstellten Sternen—:
Diese So-geliebte.

Sie aber ging an jenes Gottes Hand,
den Schritt beschränkt von langen Leichenbändern,
unsicher, sanft und ohne Ungeduld.
Sie war in sich, wie Eine hoher Hoffnung,
und dachte nicht des Mannes, der voranging,
und nicht des Weges, der ins Leben aufstieg.
Sie war in sich. Und ihr Gestorbensein
erfüllte sie wie Fülle.
Wie eine Frucht von Süßigkeit und Dunkel,
so war sie voll von ihrem großen Tode,
der also neu war, daß sie nichts begriff.

Sie war in einem neuen Mädchentum
und unberührbar; ihr Geschlecht war zu
wie eine junge Blume gegen Abend,
und ihre Hände waren der Vermählung
so sehr entwöhnt, daß selbst des leichten Gottes
unendlich leise, leitende Berührung
sie kränkte wie zu sehr Vertraulichkeit.

Sie war schon nicht mehr diese blonde Frau,
die in des Dichters Liedern manchmal anklang,
nicht mehr des breiten Bettes Duft und Eiland
und jenes Mannes Eigentum nicht mehr.

around the other earth, a sun
and a star-filled silent heaven turned,
a lament-heaven with disfigured stars—:
this one so loved.

But now she walked at that god's hand,
her stride restricted by long winding sheets,
uncertain, gentle, and without impatience.
She was within herself, like a woman rich with child,
and thought not of the man who walked ahead,
and not of the path that rose into life.
She was within herself. And her having-died
filled her like abundance.
Like a fruit full of sweetness and night,
she was full of her own great death,
which was still so new, that she grasped nothing.

She was in a new virginity
and untouchable; her sex had closed
as a young flower at approach of evening,
and her hands had been so weaned
from marriage, that even the light god's
infinitely soft, guiding touch
afflicted her like too great an intimacy.

She was no longer this blond wife,
who echoed often in the poet's songs,
no longer the wide bed's scent and island
and that man's property no longer.

Sie war schon aufgelöst wie langes Haar
und hingegeben wie gefallner Regen
und ausgeteilt wie hundertfacher Vorrat.

Sie war schon Wurzel.

Und als plötzlich jäh
der Gott sie anhielt und mit Schmerz im Ausruf
die Worte sprach: Er hat sich umgewendet— ,
begriff sie nichts und sagte leise: *Wer?*

Fern aber, dunkel vor dem klaren Ausgang,
stand irgend jemand, dessen Angesicht
nicht zu erkennen war. Er stand und sah,
wie auf dem Streifen eines Wiesenpfades
mit trauervollem Blick der Gott der Botschaft
sich schweigend wandte, der Gestalt zu folgen,
die schon zurückging dieses selben Weges,
den Schritt beschränkt von langen Leichenbändern,
unsicher, sanft und ohne Ungeduld.

She was already loosened like long hair
and given over like fallen rain
and handed out like limitless supplies.

She was already root.

And when without warning
the god stopped her and with pain in his cry
spoke the words: He has turned around—,
she grasped nothing and said softly: *Who?*

But far off, dark before the shining exit,
someone or other stood, whose features
could not be recognized. He stood and saw
how on the stripe of a meadow path
with mournful look the god of messages
turned silently around, to follow the shape
that already went back along that same path,
its stride restricted by long winding sheets,
uncertain, gentle, and without impatience.

Alkestis

Da plötzlich war der Bote unter ihnen,
hineingeworfen in das Überkochen
des Hochzeitsmahles wie ein neuer Zusatz.
Sie fühlten nicht, die Trinkenden, des Gottes
heimlichen Eintritt, welcher seine Gottheit
so an sich hielt wie einen nassen Mantel
und ihrer einer schien, der oder jener,
wie er so durchging. Aber plötzlich sah
mitten im Sprechen einer von den Gästen
den jungen Hausherrn oben an dem Tische
wie in die Höh gerissen, nicht mehr liegend,
und überall und mit dem ganzen Wesen
ein Fremdes spiegelnd, das ihn furchtbar ansprach.
Und gleich darauf, als klärte sich die Mischung,
war Stille; nur mit einem Satz am Boden
von trübem Lärm und einem Niederschlag
fallenden Lallens, schon verdorben riechend
nach dumpfem umgestandenen Gelächter.
Und da erkannten sie den schlanken Gott,
und wie er dastand, innerlich voll Sendung
und unerbittlich, —wußten sie es beinah.
Und doch, als es gesagt war, war es mehr
als alles Wissen, gar nicht zu begreifen.
Admet muß sterben. Wann? In dieser Stunde.

Der aber brach die Schale seines Schreckens
in Stücken ab und streckte seine Hände

Alcestis

Then suddenly the messenger was among them,
thrown into the simmering wedding feast
like a new ingredient. But they all
kept on drinking, and didn't feel the god's
secret entrance, as he held his godhead
tightly to him like a wet mantle
and seemed one of their own, this or that one,
as he walked through. But suddenly
in the midst of speaking one of the guests saw
the young master at the table's head
as if snatched aloft, no longer reclining,
and everywhere and with all his being
mirroring a foreignness that horribly addressed him.
And with that, as if the mixture cleared,
was stillness; only with some dregs
of muddy noise on the floor and a sediment
of falling murmur, already reeking
with the smell of muffled stagnant laughter.
And then they recognized the slender god,
and as he stood there, inwardly full of mission
and unentreatable,—they almost knew.
And yet, when it was uttered, it was more
than all knowledge, impossible to be grasped.
Admetus must die. When? Within this hour.

But he broke the shell of his fright
into pieces and stretched his hands

heraus aus ihr, um mit dem Gott zu handeln.
Um Jahre, um ein einzig Jahr noch Jugend,
um Monate, um Wochen, um paar Tage,
ach, Tage nicht, um Nächte, nur um Eine,
um Eine Nacht, um diese nur: um die.
Der Gott verneinte, und da schrie er auf
und schrie's hinaus und hielt es nicht und schrie
wie seine Mutter aufschrie beim Gebären.

Und die trat zu ihm, eine alte Frau,
und auch der Vater kam, der alte Vater,
und beide standen, alt, veraltet, ratlos,
beim Schreienden, der plötzlich, wie noch nie
so nah, sie ansah, abbrach, schluckte, sagte:
Vater,
liegt dir denn viel daran an diesem Rest,
an diesem Satz, der dich beim Schlingen hindert?
Geh, gieß ihn weg. Und du, du alte Frau,
Matrone,
was tust du denn noch hier: du hast geboren.
Und beide hielt er sie wie Opfertiere
in Einem Griff. Auf einmal ließ er los
und stieß die Alten fort, voll Einfall, strahlend
und atemholend, rufend: Kreon, Kreon!
Und nichts als das; und nichts als diesen Namen.
Aber in seinem Antlitz stand das Andere,
das er nicht sagte, namenlos erwartend,
wie ers dem jungen Freunde, dem Geliebten

out from it, to bargain with the god.
For years, for a single year more of youth,
for months, for weeks, for a few days,
ah, not days, for nights, only for *one*,
for *one* night, for this night only: for it.
The god refused, and then he screamed out loud
and screamed it out and didn't hold it and screamed
the way his mother screamed out in childbirth.

And she stepped up to him, an old woman,
and his father came too, his old father,
and both stood, old, decrepit, at a loss,
beside the screamer, who suddenly, as if never before
so near, saw them, broke off, swallowed, said:
Father,
Do you set such store on this remainder,
these dregs that choke you when you're gulping?
Go, pour them out. And you, old woman,
Mother,
what remains for you here: you've given birth.
And he held both like sacrificial beasts
in one grip. Then suddenly he let go
and shoved the old ones away, inspired, beaming
and breathing hard, calling: Creon, Creon!
And nothing else; nothing but that name.
But in his features stood that something else
he did not say, wordlessly expectant,
as he held it out glowingly to the young friend,

erglühend hinhielt übern wirren Tisch.
Die Alten (stand da), siehst du, sind kein Loskauf,
sie sind verbraucht und schlecht und beinah wertlos,
du aber, du, in deiner ganzen Schönheit—

Da aber sah er seinen Freund nicht mehr.
Er blieb zurück, und das, was kam, war *sie*,
ein wenig kleiner fast als er sie kannte
und leicht und traurig in dem bleichen Brautkleid.
Die andern alle sind nur ihre Gasse,
durch die sie kommt und kommt—: (gleich wird sie da sein
in seinen Armen, die sich schmerzhaft auftun).

Doch wie er wartet, spricht sie; nicht zu ihm.
Sie spricht zum Gotte, und der Gott vernimmt sie,
und alle hörens gleichsam erst im Gotte:

Ersatz kann keiner für ihn sein. Ich *bins*.
Ich bin Ersatz. Denn keiner ist zu Ende
wie ich es bin. Was bleibt mir denn von dem
was ich hier war? Das *ists* ja, daß ich sterbe.
Hat sie dirs nicht gesagt, da sie dirs auftrug,
daß jenes Lager, das da drinnen wartet,
zur Unterwelt gehört? Ich nahm ja Abschied.
Abschied über Abschied.
Kein Sterbender nimmt mehr davon. Ich ging ja,
damit das Alles, unter Dem begraben
der jetzt mein Gatte ist, zergeht, sich auflöst—.
So führ mich hin: ich sterbe ja für ihn.

to the loved one, across the bewildered table.
The old (it went), look, are no ransom,
they are used up and flat and almost worthless,
but you, Creon, you, in all your beauty—

But then he saw his friend no longer.
He stayed back, and that which came was *she*,
a little smaller almost than he knew her
and light and sad in her pale bridal dress.
All the others are nothing but her street,
down which she comes and comes—: (soon she'll be there
in his arms, which painfully spread open).

But as he waits, she speaks; not to him.
She speaks to the god, and the god listens,
and all hear, as if gathered in the god:

No one can stand in for him. I *am* that.
I am a stand-in. For no one is finished
the way I am. What remains to me of all
I was here? Dying *is* my life now.
Did she not tell you, when she dispatched you,
that that bed which waits there inside
belongs to the underworld? I've *said* farewell.
Farewell after farewell.
No one dying ever said more. And I've *gone*,
so that all of this, buried under Him
who is now my husband, disappears, dissolves—.
So lead me off: I *am* dying for him.

Und wie der Wind auf hoher See, der umspringt,
so trat der Gott fast wie zu einer Toten
und war auf einmal weit von ihrem Gatten,
dem er, versteckt in einem kleinen Zeichen,
die hundert Leben dieser Erde zuwarf.
Der stürzte taumelnd zu den beiden hin
und griff nach ihnen wie im Traum. Sie gingen
schon auf den Eingang zu, in dem die Frauen
verweint sich drängten. Aber einmal sah
er noch des Mädchens Antlitz, das sich wandte
mit einem Lächeln, hell wie eine Hoffnung,
die beinah ein Versprechen war: erwachsen
zurückzukommen aus dem tiefen Tode
zu ihm, dem Lebenden—

Da schlug er jäh
die Hände vors Gesicht, wie er so kniete,
um nichts zu sehen mehr nach diesem Lächeln.

And like the wind on high seas, which veers round,
the god stepped almost as toward one dead
and was suddenly far from her husband,
to whom he tossed, hidden in a small sign,
the hundred lifetimes of this earth.
The one plunged drunkenly toward the pair
and grasped at them as if in dream. They moved
already toward the entrance, where the women
crowded weeping. But just once he saw
again the girl's face, which turned
with a smile, bright like a hope
which almost was a promise: grown up
to come back from the deep death
to him, the living one—

Then suddenly he threw
his hands before his face, as he knelt there,
in order to see nothing else after that smile.

Geburt der Venus

An diesem Morgen nach der Nacht, die bang
vergangen war mit Rufen, Unruh, Aufruhr,—
brach alles Meer noch einmal auf und schrie.
Und als der Schrei sich langsam wieder schloß
und von der Himmel blassem Tag und Anfang
herabfiel in der stummen Fische Abgrund—:
gebar das Meer.

Von erster Sonne schimmerte der Haarschaum
der weiten Wogenscham, an deren Rand
das Mädchen aufstand, weiß, verwirrt und feucht.
So wie ein junges grünes Blatt sich rührt,
sich reckt und Eingerolltes langsam aufschlägt,
entfaltete ihr Leib sich in die Kühle
hinein und in den unberührten Frühwind.

Wie Monde stiegen klar die Kniee auf
und tauchten in der Schenkel Wolkenränder;
der Waden schmaler Schatten wich zurück,
die Füße spannten sich und wurden licht,
und die Gelenke lebten wie die Kehlen
von Trinkenden.

Und in dem Kelch des Beckens lag der Leib
wie eine junge Frucht in eines Kindes Hand.
In seines Nabels engem Becher war
das ganze Dunkel dieses hellen Lebens.

Birth of Venus

On this morning after the night that fearfully
had passed with outcry, tumult, uproar,—
all the sea broke open once more and screamed.
And as the scream slowly closed again
and from the sky's pale daybreak and beginning
fell down into the mute fishes' chasm—:
the sea gave birth.

The first sun shimmered in the hair-foam
of the wide wave-cleft, on whose rim
the young girl rose, white, confused, and moist.
Just as a piece of new green leaf stirs,
stretches, and something curled up slowly opens,
her body unfolded into the coolness
and into the untouched early morning wind.

Like moons the knees rose clearly
and ducked into the cloud-rims of the thighs;
the calves' slim shadows pulled back,
the feet flexed and grew luminous,
and the joints came alive like the throats
of people drinking.

And in pelvis's cup lay the belly
like a young fruit in a child's hand.
In its navel's narrow chalice was
the entire darkness of this bright life.

Darunter hob sich licht die kleine Welle
und floß beständig über nach den Lenden,
wo dann und wann ein stilles Rieseln war.
Durchschienen aber und noch ohne Schatten,
wie ein Bestand von Birken im April,
warm, leer und unverborgen, lag die Scham.

Jetzt stand der Schultern rege Waage schon
im Gleichgewichte auf dem graden Körper,
der aus dem Becken wie ein Springbrunn aufstieg
und zögernd in den langen Armen abfiel
und rascher in dem vollen Fall des Haars.

Dann ging sehr langsam das Gesicht vorbei:
aus dem verkürzten Dunkel seiner Neigung
in klares, waagrechtes Erhobensein.
Und hinter ihm verschloß sich steil das Kinn.

Jetzt, da der Hals gestreckt war wie ein Strahl
und wie ein Blumenstiel, darin der Saft steigt,
streckten sich auch die Arme aus wie Hälse
von Schwänen, wenn sie nach dem Ufer suchen.

Dann kam in dieses Leibes dunkle Frühe
wie Morgenwind der erste Atemzug.
Im zartesten Geäst der Aderbäume
entstand ein Flüstern, und das Blut begann
zu rauschen über seinen tiefen Stellen.
Und dieser Wind wuchs an: nun warf er sich

Beneath it the small wave rose lightly
and lapped continually toward the loins,
where now and then a silent ripple stirred.
But translucent and yet without shadow,
like a stand of birch trees in April,
warm, empty, and unhidden, lay the sex.

Now the shoulders' quick scales already
stood balanced on the straight body,
which rose from the pelvis like a fountain
and fell hesitantly in the long arms
and more swiftly in the hair's cascades.

Then very slowly the face went past:
from the indrawn darkness of its bending
into clear, horizontal upliftedness.
And behind it, steeply closing shut, the chin.

Now, when the neck was stretched out like a jet
and like a stalk in which the sap rises,
the arms too stretched out like necks
of swans, when they are searching for the shore.

Then into this body's dark dawning
came the first breath like morning wind.
In the vein-trees' tenderest branches
a whispering arose, and the blood began
to rush louder over its deep places.
And this wind grew on: now it hurled itself

mit allem Atem in die neuen Brüste
und füllte sie und drückte sich in sie,—
daß sie wie Segel, von der Ferne voll,
das leichte Mädchen nach dem Strande drängten.

So landete die Göttin.

Hinter ihr,
die rasch dahinschritt durch die jungen Ufer,
erhoben sich den ganzen Vormittag
die Blumen und die Halme, warm, verwirrt,
wie aus Umarmung. Und sie ging und lief.

Am Mittag aber, in der schwersten Stunde,
hob sich das Meer noch einmal auf und warf
einen Delphin an jene selbe Stelle.
Tot, rot und offen.

with all its breath into the new breasts
and filled them and pushed into them,—
so that like sails full of distance
they drove the light girl toward the shore.

And thus the goddess landed.

Behind her,
as she strode swiftly off through the young shores,
all morning the flowers and the grasses
sprang up, warm, confused,
as from embracing. And she walked and ran.

But at noon, in the heaviest hour,
the sea rose up once more and threw
a dolphin on that same spot.
Dead, red, and open.

Die Rosenschale

Zornige sahst du flackern, sahst zwei Knaben
zu einem Etwas sich zusammenballen,
das Haß war und sich auf der Erde wälzte
wie ein von Bienen überfallnes Tier;
Schauspieler, aufgetürmte Übertreiber,
rasende Pferde, die zusammenbrachen,
den Blick wegwerfend, bläkend das Gebiß
als schälte sich der Schädel aus dem Maule.

Nun aber weißt du, wie sich das vergißt:
denn vor dir steht die volle Rosenschale,
die unvergeßlich ist und angefüllt
mit jenem Äußersten von Sein und Neigen,
Hinhalten, Niemals-Gebenkönnen, Dastehn,
das unser sein mag: Äußerstes auch uns.

Lautloses Leben, Aufgehn ohne Ende,
Raum-brauchen ohne Raum von jenem Raum
zu nehmen, den die Dinge rings verringern,
fast nicht Umrissen-sein wie Ausgespartes
und lauter Inneres, viel seltsam Zartes
und Sich-bescheinendes—bis an den Rand:
ist irgend etwas uns bekannt wie dies?

Und dann wie dies: daß ein Gefühl entsteht,
weil Blütenblätter Blütenblätter rühren?
Und dies: daß eins sich aufschlägt wie ein Lid,
und drunter liegen lauter Augenlider,

The Bowl of Roses

You saw anger flare, saw two boys
ball themselves into something
that was hatred and writhed on the ground
like an animal attacked by bees;
actors, towering exaggerators,
raging horses that crashed down,
casting away their gazes, baring their teeth
as if their skulls peeled from their mouths.

But now you know how that's forgotten:
before you stands the full bowl of roses,
which is unforgettable and filled
with that utmost of being and bending,
holding out, lacking power to give, standing here,
that might be ours: the utmost for us as well.

Soundless living, endless opening out,
space being used without space being taken
from that space adjacent things diminish,
existence almost uncontoured, like ground left blank
and pure within-ness, much so strangely soft
and self-illuminating—out to the edge:
is there anything we know like this?

And then like this: that a feeling begins,
because flower petals touch flower petals?
And this: that one opens like a lid,
and under it lie only eyelids,

geschlossene, als ob sie, zehnfach schlafend,
zu dämpfen hätten eines Innern Sehkraft.
Und dies vor allem: daß durch diese Blätter
das Licht hindurch muß. Aus den tausend Himmeln
filtern sie langsam jenen Tropfen Dunkel,
in dessen Feuerschein das wirre Bündel
der Staubgefäße sich erregt und aufbäumt.

Und die Bewegung in den Rosen, sieh:
Gebärden von so kleinem Ausschlagswinkel,
daß sie unsichtbar blieben, liefen ihre
Strahlen nicht auseinander in das Weltall.

Sieh jene weiße, die sich selig aufschlug
und dasteht in den großen offnen Blättern
wie eine Venus aufrecht in der Muschel;
und die errötende, die wie verwirrt
nach einer kühlen sich hinüberwendet,
und wie die kühle fühllos sich zurückzieht,
und wie die kalte steht, in sich gehüllt,
unter den offenen, die alles abtun.
Und *was* sie abtun, wie das leicht und schwer,
wie es ein Mantel, eine Last, ein Flügel
und eine Maske sein kann, je nach dem,
und *wie* sie's abtun: wie vor dem Geliebten.

Was können sie nicht sein: war jene gelbe,
die hohl und offen daliegt, nicht die Schale
von einer Frucht, darin dasselbe Gelb,

all closed, as if they, sleeping tenfold,
had to damp an inner power of sight.
And this above all: that through these petals
light must pass. Out of the thousand skies
they slowly filter that drop of darkness
within whose fiery glow the tangled bunch
of stamens trembles and rears erect.

And the movement in the roses, look:
gestures from such small angles of deflection
that they'd remain invisible, if their
rays did not fan out into the universe.

Look at that white one which blissfully unfolded
and stands there in the great open petals
like a Venus upright in the seashell;
and the blushing one, which as if confused
turns across to one that is cool,
and how that cold one stands, wrapped in itself,
among the open ones that shed everything.
And *what* they shed: how it can be
light and heavy, a cloak, a burden, a wing
and a mask, it varies endlessly,
and *how* they shed it: as before the loved one.

What can't they be: was that yellow one,
which lies there hollow and open, not the rind
of a fruit, in which the very same yellow,

gesammelter, orangeröter, Saft war?
Und wars für diese schon zu viel, das Aufgehn,
weil an der Luft ihr namenloses Rosa
den bittern Nachgeschmack des Lila annahm?
Und die batistene, ist sie kein Kleid,
in dem noch zart und atemwarm das Hemd streckt,
mit dem zugleich es abgeworfen wurde
im Morgenschatten an dem alten Waldbad?
Und diese hier, opalnes Porzellan,
zerbrechlich, eine flache Chinatasse
und angefüllt mit kleinen hellen Faltern,—
und jene da, die nichts enthält als sich.

Und sind nicht alle so, nur sich enthaltend,
wenn Sich-enthalten heißt: die Welt da draußen
und Wind und Regen und Geduld des Frühlings
und Schuld und Unruh und vermummtes Schicksal
und Dunkelheit der abendlichen Erde
bis auf der Wolken Wandel, Flucht und Anflug,
bis auf den vagen Einfluß ferner Sterne
in eine Hand voll Innres zu verwandeln.

Nun liegt es sorglos in den offnen Rosen.

more collected, orange-redder, was juice?
And was opening-out too much for this one,
since in the air its indescribable pink
took on the bitter aftertaste of violet?
And that cambric one, is it not a dress
in which, still soft and breath-warm, the chemise
clings, both of them cast off at once
in the morning shadows of the old forest pool?
And this one, opalescent porcelain,
fragile, a shallow china cup
and filled with tiny bright butterflies,—
and that one, which contains nothing but itself.

And aren't all that way, containing just themselves,
if self-containing means: to change the world outside
and wind and rain and patience of the spring
and guilt and restlessness and muffled fate
and the darkness of the evening earth
out to the changing and flying and fleeing of the clouds
and the vague influence of distant stars
into a hand full of inwardness.

Now it lies carefree in these open roses.

Design by David Bullen
Typeset in Mergenthaler Fournier
by Wilsted & Taylor
Printed by Maple-Vail